God's Healing team
Instruction for healing God's way

Jer 33:3 NKJV 'Call to Me, and I will answer you, and show you great and mighty things, which you do not know.'

By Rev. Judith S. Johnson

Xulon
PRESS

God's Healing Team
Instruction for healing God's way
by Rev. Judith S. Johnson
Phone # 618.632.7983
Judithofallon@aol.com

Printed in the United States of America

ISBN 9781613798485

www.xulonpress.com

Dedication

◇◁

To My Best Friend
The Holy Spirit
He's My Guiding Light. Everything
good that I do comes from Him.

To My Second Best Friend
Barbara (Bobbie Woods)
She Used to Be My Student,
Now She is My Minister
An Awesome Woman of God

To All of God's Chosen People
Those He Used to Train Me

To God's Healing Team
The Originals
Deborah Cataldo
Sharon Smith
Susan Foster

These Ladies asked me to teach them. At that time I was at a very low place in my Ministry and I really wasn't sure what I had to offer. God let me know I was supposed to do it so we went forth. Their excitement, honesty and rapid growth gave me courage and was instrumental in giving me back the confidence I had lost. I will be forever grateful for their friendship and their faith in me.

Table of Content

◇⋈

Introduction

◇✕

2 Peter 1:1-11

1:1 Simon Peter, a servant and apostle of Jesus Christ, To those who through the righteousness of our God and Savior Jesus Christ have received a faith as precious as ours: 2 Grace and peace be yours in abundance through the knowledge of God and of Jesus our Lord. 3 **His divine power has given us everything we need for life and godliness** through our knowledge of him who called us by his own glory and goodness. 4 Through these he has given us his very great and precious promises, so that through them **you may participate in the divine nature** and escape the corruption in the world caused by evil desires. 5 For this very reason, make every effort to add to your faith goodness; and to goodness, knowledge; 6 and to knowledge, self-control; and to self-control, perseverance; and to perseverance, godliness; 7 and to godliness, brotherly kindness; and to brotherly kindness, love. 8 For if you possess these qualities in increasing measure, they will keep you from being ineffective and unproductive in your knowledge of our Lord Jesus Christ. 9 But if anyone does not have them, he is nearsighted and blind, and has forgotten that he has been cleansed from his past sins. 10 Therefore, my brothers, be all the more eager to make your calling and election sure. For **if you do these things, you**

will never fall, 11 and you will receive a rich welcome into the eternal kingdom of our Lord and Savior Jesus Christ. NIV

ASK GOD

In the beginning of my Christian walk God would put questions in my head. I thought this is something He did with everyone. I would hear things like, "God should I go up for prayer" at the end of the church service? I automatically knew if I heard "yes", I would receive healing. If I heard "no", I knew it was pointless to go. Then I heard, "God what should I wear today? or what should I cook for supper?" After a while it became automatic because I found out when I asked I had success.

I prayed and asked God, Father, please always give me the questions to ask. Through these God questions I have learned to receive His input into many situations, whether personal or for others. This process is not a game. I take it seriously and I don't use it frivolously. I have also learned to take an extra moment to focus on Him before making serious decisions. That alone has saved me from making serious mistakes.

Jer 33:3 NKJV
'Call to Me, and I will answer you, and show you great and mighty things, which you do not now.'

I believe there is a process to achieving success in God. I want you to learn the process and open your mind and heart to the endless possibilities open to those who will dare to take Him out of the "box" and give Him the freedom to work through you. I want you to know it will be scriptural and agape love based.

Basics

✗

Jesus... (Jehovah is salvation)
The Holy Spirit will come upon you and the power of the Most High will overshadow you.
Christ...(anointed one)
anoint...1. to apply oil, ointment or a similar substance to.
2. to put oil on during a religious ceremony as a sign of sanctification or consecration.

I believe that when we were "Born Again" the Holy Spirit (the power of God) overshadows us just like He did with Mary and plants the seed of Jesus along with the anointing that is in Him into our spirit, thus planting the divine nature along with the endless possibilities and capabilities of God's power in us.

Eph 3:20-21 NKJV
20 Now to Him who is able to do exceedingly abundantly above all that we ask or think, **according to the power that works in us,** 21 to Him be glory in the church by Christ Jesus to all generations, forever and ever. Amen.

John 5:1-23 NKJV
5:1 **A Man Healed at the Pool of Bethesda** After this there was a feast of the Jews, and Jesus went up to Jerusalem. 2

Now there is in Jerusalem by the Sheep Gate a pool, which is called in Hebrew, Bethesda, having five porches. 3 In these lay a great multitude of sick people, blind, lame, paralyzed, waiting for the moving of the water. **4 For an angel went down at a certain time into the pool and stirred up the water; then whoever stepped in first, after the stirring of the water, was made well of whatever disease he had.** 5 Now a certain man was there who had an infirmity thirty-eight years. 6 When Jesus saw him lying there, and knew that he already had been in that condition a long time, He said to him, "Do you want to be made well?" 7 The sick man answered Him, "Sir, I have no man to put me into the pool when the water is stirred up; but while I am coming, another steps down before me." 8 Jesus said to him, "Rise, take up your bed and walk." 9 And immediately the man was made well, took up his bed, and walked. And that day was the Sabbath. 10 The Jews therefore said to him who was cured, "It is the Sabbath; it is not lawful for you to carry your bed." 11 He answered them, "He who made me well said to me, 'Take up your bed and walk.'" 12 Then they asked him, "Who is the Man who said to you, 'Take up your bed and walk'?" 13 But the one who was healed did not know who it was, for Jesus had withdrawn, a multitude being in that place. 14 Afterward Jesus found him in the temple, and said to him, "See, you have been made well. Sin no more, lest a worse thing come upon you." 15 The man departed and told the Jews that it was Jesus who had made him well. 16 Honor the Father and the Son For this reason the Jews persecuted Jesus, and sought to kill Him, because He had done these things on the Sabbath. 17 But Jesus answered them, "My Father has been working until now, and I have been working." 18 Therefore the Jews sought all the more to kill Him, because He not only broke the Sabbath, but also said that God was His Father, making Himself equal with God. 19 Then Jesus answered and said to them, "Most assuredly, I say to you, **the Son can do nothing of Himself, but what He sees the Father do; for whatever He does, the Son also does in like manner. 20 For the Father loves the Son, and shows Him all things that He Himself does; and He will show Him greater works than these, that you may marvel.** 21 For as the Father raises the dead and gives life to them, even so the Son gives life to whom He will. 22 For the Father judges no one, but has committed all judgment to the Son, 23 that all should honor the Son just as they honor the Father. He who does not honor the Son does not honor the Father who sent Him.

Chapter One introduction

◇◁

In this chapter I am giving you scripture reference and the meaning of the things we should know as Christians. I have found that we already are doing them but most don't know why. They just do them because that is what we are told to do.

Salvation Scriptures
Two Salvation Sample Prayers with Confession
Definition of the word saved.
Communion... The Love Feast

The Blood scriptures to Honor Jesus for the benefits

The Lord's Supper scriptures

You are a Blood Brother to Jesus Christ

Chapter One

Keep the first things first

❖

No one can see the Kingdom of God unless he is "Born Again," it is as simple as that. You cannot enter into the spiritual realm which is the Kingdom in which God lives unless you are "Born again." In order to be a part of His healing Ministry, you must do it His way.

If you have not asked Jesus into your heart and to become the Lord of your life, now is your opportunity.

This book is meant for the Christian that is ready to step out in Ministry.

Salvation Scriptures

John 3:3 NIV
3 In reply Jesus declared, "I tell you the truth, no one can see the kingdom of God unless he is born again."

Acts 16:29-31 NIV
29 The jailer called for lights, rushed in and fell trembling before Paul and Silas. 30 He then brought them out and asked, "Sirs, what must I do to be saved?" 31 They replied, "Believe in the Lord Jesus, and you will be saved — you and your household."

Rev 3:20 NIV
20 Here I am! I stand at the door and knock. If anyone hears my voice and opens the door, I will come in and eat with him, and he with me.

Rom 10:9-11 NIV
9 That if you confess with your mouth, "Jesus is Lord," and believe in your heart that God raised him from the dead, you will be saved. 10 For it is with your heart that you believe and are justified, and it is with your mouth that you confess and are saved.

2 Cor 1:20-22 NIV
21 Now it is God who makes both us and you stand firm in Christ. He anointed us, 22 set his seal of ownership on us, and put his Spirit in our hearts as a deposit, guaranteeing what is to come.

Salvation Prayer

Father, Please forgive me for all my sins. I forgive all those who have trespassed against me.

Jesus, I believe you are the Son of God. You came to earth, lived as a man, went to the cross, died for my sins and was raised from the dead by the Holy Spirit. Please come into my heart and be the Lord of my life. Help me be become all I can be through you. Teach me to love other people and to lead a life that will make you proud to call me a Christian.

........Confession........

I am a Born again Christian and Jesus is my Lord.

When a person comes to you for healing it may be the only opportunity you will have to Minister to them. First, ask them if they are "Born Again." If the answer is yes go ahead but if they don't know or if the answer is no, ask if they would like to say that prayer and be positive they are. Not just for where they will go when they die but for the benefits they will receive while they are on this earth. Remember, their Spiritual healing is even more important than their physical healing.

Another Sample Prayer

Ask them,

   Do you believe the Easter story? Do you believe Jesus, the Son of God came to earth, lived as a man, went to the cross, died for your sins and on the third day was raised from the dead by the Holy Spirit.

   Please repeat after me,

Father, I come to you in Jesus Name. Please forgive me for all my sins. I forgive all those who have sinned against me. In Jesus name.

Jesus, I ask you to come into my heart and be the Lord of my life. Make me what you want me to be. Thank you I am a "Born Again" Christian.

Make them aware of what being saved means.

Save. A Verb which means it's always on the move. It never stagnates. Does not stand still.

1. To rescue from harm, danger or loss. To set free from the consequences of sin.
2. To keep in a safe condition. Safeguard.
3. to prevent the waste or loss of.
4. to set aside for future use; Store.
5. To treat with care by avoiding fatigue, wear or damage.

Communion
(The Love Feast)

In 1 Cor 11:17-34 Paul rebuked the Corinthians for their pride and greed during the meal that accompanied the Eucharist (v 17-22). Then (v 23-25) he describes the institution of the Lord's Supper and emphasized the need for Christians to partake in a worthy manner. Yes, get rid of the sin but most of all see the wonders of what He accomplished. Many of them that had not been doing so were weak and sick, and many had even died as a result of God's judgment(v 27-34). They did not recognize or celebrate the benefits He provided for us by going to the cross. They did not recognize healing was for them.

First, the Lord's supper is a time of remembrance and thanksgiving. Jesus said, "Do this in remembrance of me"(Luke 22:19; 1 Cor 11:24-25). We are to recognize His sacrifice but we are not to dwell on the agonies of His crucifixion as much as remembering His wonderful life and ministry and the gifts He provided for us on that cross. This is a time to honor our Lord, showing our appreciation and expressing our deepest praise for all He has done and accomplished.

Second, this is our moment in time to commune with our Lord and Savior. Draw closer and show Him your love. We are participating in the benefits of Jesus' death and resurrection to life. (Rom 5:10; 1 Cor 10:16) We are actually being nourished and empowered by the Holy Spirit every time we do this.

Third, This supper is a time of commitment and anticipation. We are to examine our-selves and receive in a worthy manner (1 Cor 11:28-29), from a clear conscience and with forgiveness in our hearts toward others. Renewing our dedication to Christ and His people, in anticipation until He comes (1 Cor 11:26)

The Blood
Honor Him for the benefits

We have the "Mind of Christ" through the Blood. Col 1:20
We are the "Righteousness of God" through faith in the Blood of Jesus Christ. Rom 3:22-25
We have "Peace" through the Blood of Jesus Christ. Col 1:20
We have forgiveness of sins because of the Blood. Matt 26:28
We have eternal life through the Blood of Jesus Christ. John 6:54
We are Justified (Just as if we'd never sinned) by His Blood. Rom 5:9-11
We are brought near to God by the Blood of Jesus. Eph 2:13
We are redeemed by the Blood. Heb 9:12
The Blood of Jesus cleanses our consciences from acts that lead to death. Heb 9:14
We enter the Most Holy place by the Blood of Jesus. Heb 10:19
We are made Holy through the Blood of Jesus. Heb 13:12
The Blood of Jesus purifies us from all sin. 1 John 1:7
We have overcome Satan by the Blood of the Lamb. Rev 12:11
We have all the fullness of the Trinity dwelling in us through the Blood of Jesus. Col 1:15-21

Salvation
Purchased for us by Jesus Blood

SOZO (Greek)... Material and Temporal deliverance from danger, suffering, etc.
save...verb. A Verb which means it's filled with power and always on the move.
1. To rescue from harm, danger or loss. To set free from the consequences of sin.

2. To keep in a safe condition. Safeguarded through the Blood.
3. To prevent the waste or loss of.
4. To set aside for future use; Store.
5. To treat with care.

The Lord's Supper

Matt 26:26-29 NKJV
And as they were eating, Jesus took bread, blessed and broke it, and gave it to the disciples and said, "Take, eat; this is My body."

27 Then He took the cup, and gave thanks, and gave it to them, saying, "Drink from it, all of you. 28 For this is My blood of the new covenant, which is shed for many for the remission of sins.

You are a Blood Brother to Jesus Christ

Chapter Two introduction

◇<

There is some controversy concerning this subject. Some Churches believe that the Baptism in the Holy Spirit with the evidence of speaking in other tongues is "not for today." That saddens me because it is a form of rejection to the Holy Spirit. I will not try to convince you to receive it but I will challenge you to ask God directly if He wants you to have it. **"God, if you want me to receive the Holy Spirit and speak in tongues then please Baptize me in the Holy Spirit with the evidence of speaking in other tongues."**

**Baptism. Jewish Baptism. Johns Baptism.
Baptism of Jesus.**

We are Baptized into Christ Jesus

**Jesus said, "Go into all the world and preach
the gospel to every creature"**

My Commitment

There is a Second Baptism in Scripture

I will pour out My Spirit on all flesh;

The seven Spirits of God

Empowered for the work

Mandated by Jesus
(These signs will follow those who believe)
Mark 16:15-18 NKJV

Purpose of Tongues

Speaks mysteries
Magnifying God
Edifying ourselves
Building yourselves up
Praying in the Spirit
Allowing our spirits to have contact
with God's Spirit
The Apostles did it, I will do it.
Devotional Gift

Prayer to receive the Holy Spirit

Chapter Two

Water Baptism
Baptism in the Holy Ghost

Baptism. The application of water as a rite of purification or initiation; The word Baptism is the English form of the Greek word baptismos. The verb from which this noun is derived-baptizo- is held by some scholars to mean "to dip, immerse."

Jewish Baptism. Baptisms or ceremonial purification, were common among the Jews. Not only priests and other persons but also clothing, utensils, articles of furniture were also ceremonially cleansed. (Lev 8:6; Ex 19:10-14; Mark 7:3; Heb 9:10).

Johns Baptism. The Baptism of John was not Christian, but Jewish. It was, however, a baptism "for repentance." The only faith it expressed concerning Christ was that His coming was close at hand. Those who confessed and repented of their sins and were baptized by John were thus obedient to His call to "make ready the way of the Lord (Matt 3:3)."

Baptism of Jesus. The baptism of Jesus received from John was unique in its meaning and purpose. It could not be like what he administered to others, for Jesus did not make confession; He had no reason to repent. It was an act of ceremonial righteousness appropriate to His public entrance into His mission as the Christ, which included His threefold office of Prophet, Priest and King. The Levitical law required all the priests to be consecrated when they were about thirty years of age (Num 4:3; Luke 3:23). The consecration was twofold-first the washing (Baptism), then the anointing (Ex 29:4-7; Lev 8:36). When John on the Bank of the Jordan "washed" (baptized) Jesus, The heavens were opened and the Holy Spirit came upon Him. This was the Priestly anointing of Him who was not only a priest by divine appointment but an eternal Priest (Ps 110:4) who was divinely consecrated for the work of redemption (Matt 3:16; Acts 4:27; 10:38).

The office of Christ was and is to baptize with the Holy Ghost. His disciples administered the symbolical baptism.

Jesus' Water Baptism

Matt 3:13-17 NKJV
13 John Baptizes Jesus
Then Jesus came from Galilee to John at the Jordan to be baptized by him. 14 And John tried to prevent Him, saying, "I need to be baptized by You, and are You coming to me?"
15 But Jesus answered and said to him, "Permit it to be so now, for thus it is fitting for us to fulfill all righteousness." Then he allowed Him.
16 When He had been baptized, Jesus came up immediately from the water; and behold, the heavens were opened to Him, and He saw the Spirit of God descending like a dove and alighting upon Him. 17 And suddenly a voice came from heaven, saying, "This is My beloved Son, in whom I am well pleased."

This set of Scriptures shows us the Trinity working together

Baptized into Christ Jesus

Rom 6:3-6 NKJV
3 Or do you not know that as many of us as were **baptized into Christ Jesus** were baptized into His death? 4 Therefore we were buried with Him through baptism into death, that just as Christ was raised from the dead by the glory of the Father, even so we also should walk in newness of life. 5 For if we have been united together in the likeness of His death, certainly we also shall be in the likeness of His resurrection, 6 knowing this, that our old man was crucified with Him, that the body of sin might be done away with, that we should no longer be slaves of sin.

"I believe that Jesus Christ is the Son of God."

Acts 8:36-37 NKJV
36 Now as they went down the road, they came to some water. And the eunuch said, "See, here is water. What hinders me from being baptized?" 37 Then Philip said, "If you believe with all your heart, you may." And he answered and said, **"I believe that Jesus Christ is the Son of God."**

Jesus said, "Go into all the world and preach the gospel to every creature"

Mark 16:15-18 NKJV
15 And He said to them, "Go into all the world and preach the gospel to every creature. 16 He who believes and is baptized will be saved; but he who does not believe will be condemned. 17 **And these signs will follow those who believe: In My name they will cast out demons; they will**

speak with new tongues; 18 they will take up serpents; and if they drink anything deadly, it will by no means hurt them; they will lay hands on the sick, and they will recover."

Jesus was publicly Baptized as the example to follow. When you are baptized you are making a public statement of dedication and commitment as a Christian.

My Commitment
I believe that Jesus is the Son of God. As He was Baptized, I choose to be Baptized into Christ Jesus. I will go where He sends me and proudly confess His name. In Jesus name I will **cast out demons: I will speak with new tongues: I will take up serpents; ("to send them into the dry places") and if I** drink anything deadly, it will by no means hurt me. I **will lay hands on the sick**, and they will recover. In Jesus Name

There is a second Baptism in Scripture. There are Churches who deny it saying that it was for yesterday and not for today. He is the same yesterday, today and forever. You must be "Born Again" but it is a choice to speak in tongues. The seven-fold Spirit of God is available to you through the Baptism in the Holy Spirit giving you all the power you need to be effective in the Ministry. If you have not received this Baptism of fire, I challenge you to ask God if He wants you to speak in tongues and If He does to Baptize you.

I will pour out My Spirit on all flesh;
Foretold in the Old Testament

Joel 2:28-29 NKJV
28 God's Spirit Poured Out "And it shall come to pass afterward That **I will pour out My Spirit on all flesh;** Your sons

and your daughters shall prophesy, Your old men shall dream dreams, Your young men shall see visions. 29 And also on My menservants and on My maidservants I will pour out My Spirit in those days.

The seven Spirits of God

Rev 3:1 NKJV
3:1 The Dead Church "And to the angel of the church in Sardis write, 'These things says **He who has the seven Spirits of God** and the seven stars: "I know your works, that you have a name that you are alive, but you are dead

Isa 11:2 NKJV
2 The Spirit of the LORD shall rest upon Him, The Spirit of wisdom and understanding, The Spirit of counsel and might, The Spirit of knowledge and of the fear of the LORD.

Empowered for the work

John 14:12-17 NKJV
12 The Answered Prayer
"Most assuredly, I say to you, **he who believes in Me, the works that I do he will do also; and greater works than these he will do, because I go to My Father.** 13 **And whatever you ask in My name, that I will do,** that the Father may be glorified in the Son. 14 If you ask anything in My name, I will do it. 15 "If you love Me, keep My commandments. **16 And I will pray the Father, and He will give you another Helper, that He may abide with you forever — 17 the Spirit of truth, whom the world cannot receive, because it neither sees Him nor knows Him; but you know Him, for He dwells with you and will be in you.**

Mandated by Jesus
(Will follow those who believe)

Mark 16:15-18 NKJV
15 And He said to them, "Go into all the world and preach the gospel to every creature. 16 He who believes and is baptized will be saved; but he who does not believe will be condemned. 17 And these signs will follow those who believe: In My name they will cast out demons; they will speak with new tongues; 18 they will take up serpents; and if they drink anything deadly, it will by no means hurt them; they will lay hands on the sick, and they will recover."

Purpose of Tongues
Initial evidence of receiving the Holy Spirit

Acts 2:4 NKJV
4 And they were all filled with the Holy Spirit and began to speak with other tongues, as the Spirit gave them utterance.

Speaks mysteries
You are praying in all the wonderful things
God wants for you.

1 Cor 14:2 NKJV
2 For he who speaks in a tongue does not speak to men but to God, for no one understands him; however, in the spirit he **speaks mysteries**.

Magnifying God

Acts 10:45-46 NKJV
45 And those of the circumcision who believed were astonished, as many as came with Peter, because the gift of the

Holy Spirit had been poured out on the Gentiles also. 46 For they heard them speak with tongues and magnify God.

Edifying ourselves

1 Cor 14:4 NKJV
4 He who speaks in a tongue **edifies himself**, but he who prophesies edifies the church.

1 Cor 14:5 NKJV
Paul said, "5 **I wish you all spoke with tongues**,"

Building yourselves up

Jude 20 NKJV
But you, beloved**, building yourselves up on your most holy faith, praying in the Holy Spirit,**

Praying in the Spirit

Eph 6:18 NKJV
18 praying always with all prayer and supplication **in the Spirit**, being watchful to this end with all perseverance and supplication for all the saints

Allowing our spirits to have contact with God's Spirit

Heb 12:9 NKJV
9 Furthermore, we have had human fathers who corrected us, and we paid them respect. Shall we not much more readily be in subjection to the Father of spirits and live?

1 Cor 14:14 NKJV
14 For if I pray in a tongue, my spirit prays, but my understanding is unfruitful.

What this is saying is that when in your tongues, the Holy Spirit is giving the utterance and your mind is not involved. It bypasses your intellect meaning you don't engage your brain, just your mouth.

The Apostles did it, I will do it.

Eph 2:19-22 NKJV
Now, therefore, you are no longer strangers and foreigners, but fellow citizens with the saints and members of the household of God, 20 having been **built on the foundation of the apostles and prophets, Jesus Christ Himself being the chief cornerstone**, 21 in whom the whole building, being fitted together, grows into a holy temple in the Lord, 22 in whom **you also are being built together for a dwelling place of God in the Spirit.**

Devotional Gift
Used in prayer, praise and worship to the Father. Paul explains there is a difference between your personal prayer language communicating with God as opposed to the gift used in Church.

1 Cor 14:18 NKJV
18 I thank my God I speak with tongues more than you all; 19 yet in the church I would rather speak five words with my understanding, that I may teach others also, than ten thousand words in a tongue.

Receiving the Holy Spirit

Pray or ask someone else to pray.......
Heavenly Father, Your Word says.......

Mark 16:17 NKJV
17 And these signs will follow those who believe: In My name they will cast out demons; they will speak with new tongues;
   and
Acts 2:4 NKJV
4 And they were all filled with the Holy Spirit and began to **speak with other tongues, as the Spirit gave them utterance.**

According to your Word, please fill me with the Holy Spirit with the evidence of speaking in other tongues. In Jesus Name

Now speak out in your heavenly language and praise the Lord for His wonderful gift. The more you use your tongues the stronger you will get. It's like a Spiritual Bank account.

Chapter Three introduction

✦

G od doesn't need you to do the job. It is a privilege to be chosen. He could raise up a donkey. Keep your pride in check, keep Jesus in focus and just do what He is calling you to do with each person you Minister to and with.

Of One Mind, With One Purpose

Trying to Do the Job Alone

Don't Get Puffed Up Or You Could Have
A Rude Awakening

Example: Speak the Scripture into your life.

Thoughts to ponder

My confession
(: I AM.................BY FAITH :)

It's easy to act right when you are in Church.

THE BUMPER STICKER

Chapter Three

Attitude
The Love Walk

<><

W hen I was a child I thought like a child. Now that I'm
an adult I try very hard to think and act as an adult.
It's not always easy, it is an ongoing process. Becoming an
adult begins with the mind. We must be educated before we
can be expected to see things with logic, in this case God
logic. His logic begins and ends with compassion and Agape
love.

If I know what is expected of me and what the guidelines
and boundaries are I will do my best to remain within the
area designated to me.

We should not teach doctrine. speak Jesus and the love
of God to everyone. We don't have time to get into lengthy
teachings, our purpose is to heal. Keep in mind that this may
be the only time we will have the opportunity to speak Jesus
to those sitting in front of us. Focus on the Holy Spirit and
His leading to plant the seeds He wants planted.

Of One Mind, With One Purpose
We are blessed to be associated with an organization
having a variety of personalities with the varied backgrounds

needed to reach every person God brings into our meetings, but when there is strife between us it hinders the Holy Spirit from operating to the fullness He intends. **The only star is Jesus**. Our aim is to be "filled with and led by the Holy Spirit," working as a team. Everyone wins when we go in with a prayed up, God directed attitude. The following was given to us at a Kenneth Hagin Ministers Conference letting us know the consequences of acting on our own.

Trying to Do the Job Alone
Author unknown

Dear Sir:

I am writing in response to your request for additional information for my insurance claim. In block number three of the accident claim form I wrote, "trying to do the job alone" as the cause of the accident. You said in your letter that I should explain that statement more fully. I trust the following details will be sufficient.

I am a bricklayer by trade. On the date of the accident I was working on the roof of a new six story building. When I completed my work I discovered I had about 500 pounds of bricks left over. Rather than carrying the bricks down by hand I decided to lower them in a barrel by using a pulley which was attached to the side of the building at the sixed floor level.

Securing the rope at ground level, I went up to the roof, swung the barrel out and loaded the bricks into it. Then I went back and untied the rope, holding it tightly to insure a slow decent of the 500 pounds of bricks. You will note in block 22 of the claim form that my weight is 150 pounds. Due to my surprise at being jerked off the ground so suddenly, I lost my presence of mind and forgot to let go of the rope. Needless to say, I proceeded up the side of the building at a very rapid rate of speed. In the vicinity of the third floor I met the barrel coming down. This explains my fractured skull and collarbone. Slowed only slightly, I continued my rapid ascent, not stopping until the fingers of my right hand were two knuckles deep in the pulley.

By this time, I had regained my presence of mind and was able to hold tightly to the rope in spite of my pain. At approximately the same time however, the barrel of bricks hit the ground and the bottom fell out of the barrel. Devoid of the weight of the bricks the barrel then weighed approximately 50 pounds.

I refer you again to the information in block number 22 regarding my weight. As you might imagine, I began a rapid decent down the side of the building, In the vicinity of the third floor I met the barrel coming up. This accounts for the two fractured ankles and the lacerations of my legs and lower body.

The second encounter with the barrel slowed me enough to lessen my injuries when I fell into the pile of bricks, and fortunately, only three vertebrae were cracked, I am sorry to report, however, as I lay there on the bricks in pain, unable to stand, and watching the empty barrel six stories above me, I again lost my presence of mind and let go of the rope. The empty barrel weighed more that the rope so it came down upon me and broke both my legs.

I hope I have furnished information sufficient to explain why "trying to do the job alone " was the stated cause of the accident.

Sincerely, A Bricklayer

DON'T GET PUFFED UP OR YOU COULD HAVE A RUDE AWAKENING

1 Cor 13:1-8 NIV

13:1 If I speak in the tongues of men and of angels, but have not love, I am only a resounding gong or a clanging cymbal. 2 If I have the gift of prophecy and can fathom all mysteries and all knowledge, and if I have a faith that can move mountains, but have not love, I am nothing. 3 If I give all I possess to the poor and surrender my body to the flames, but have not love, I gain nothing.

Love is known only by the actions it prompts. God's love gives. It gave His Son. He loved us first. His love is a deliberate choice. Even when it cost him. That love was and is displayed in the person of Jesus Christ. Christ like love is produced in the Christian by the Holy Spirit. As we yield to God and study His word our thinking changes because we begin to see others through His eyes. That was how Jesus could say, "Father forgive them, they know not what they do." They really do not understand the depth of what they are doing. These things can only be discerned by the Spirit of God. As God made a deliberate choice to love us first, can we do the same for others.

Agape love, God's love is not based on feelings. It is a decision to love. It actively looks for opportunity to do good and works no ill will toward anyone. I obviously have not reached the standard of love demonstrated by our Heavenly Father or Jesus, **but I have made the choice** and have spoken the word's, "I choose to love."

In the beginning God created the Heavens and the earth, He spoke the world into existence when He said, "let there be light." and then there was light. Now speak your words of love into existence and watch God bring them to pass.

Example: Speak the Scripture into your life.

My love is patient, My love is kind. I do not envy, I do not boast, I am not proud. I am not rude, I am not self-seeking, I am not easily angered, I do not keep a record of wrongs. My Love does not delight in evil but rejoices with the truth. My Love always protects, My Love always trusts,

My Love always hopes, My Love always perseveres. My Love never fails.

— — — — —Thoughts to ponder— — — — — —

1 Cor 3:16-17 NKJV
16 Do you not know that you are the temple of God and that the Spirit of God dwells in you? 17 If anyone defiles the temple of God, God will destroy him. For the temple of God is holy, which temple you are.

2 Cor 3:17-18 NKJV
17 Now the Lord is the Spirit; and where the Spirit of the Lord is, there is liberty.

Are you seeing others as the temple of God?
Are you treating them with respect?
Are you teaching them that true freedom only comes with a personal relationship with Jesus Christ?
Are you aware that God see's them through the eyes of faith, not only as they are, but as they will become?
Are you aware that God see's you the same way?
After you have Ministered to them, do they know that they are special in God's eye's or do they see Him standing over them with a baseball bat waiting for them to make a mistake so He can beat them up?

Are you thought of as a winner? I want to be. Unfortunately there are a lot of Christians running around whose reputation is more of a flake than that of a winner. I have made an active decision. I want to be a person that people can trust. One that they can call on when they are hurting. In order for that to happen I have to build a reputation that God will be proud of.

1 Cor 15:58 NKJV
58 Therefore, my beloved brethren, be steadfast, immovable, always abounding in the work of the Lord, knowing that your labor is not in vain in the Lord.

The word immovable in the Greek is ametakinetos, which has several meanings.
1. It means not easily excited, shaken or effected.
2. Something that is not changeable or unpredictable.
3. used in referring to stone structures.
4. A building, person or place that is constant, stable, enduring and dependable.

This is the way I want to be described. A person that God can trust to carry out the work He is calling me to.

My confession
(: I AM...............BY FAITH :)

I choose to love through God.
I am not easily excited, shaken or effected.
I am not changeable or unpredictable.
I am built upon the rock.
I am constant, stable, enduring and dependable.

Now, when you have reached this stature, remember that God hates a haughty spirit. :)
        It's easy to act right when you are in Church.

THE BUMPER STICKER
Author unknown

The man explains,

I was sitting at a stop light this morning. The lady in front of me was going through some papers on the seat of her car and when the light changed she did not obey it's command.... A green light is a command not a suggestion.

When the light turned red and she still did not move, I began (with my windows rolled up) screaming epithets and beating on my steering wheel. My expressions of distress were interrupted by a policeman, gun drawn, tapping on my window. Against my protestations of, "you can't arrest me for hollering in my car." He ordered me into the back seat of his.

After about two hours in a holding cell, the arresting officer advised, you are free to go. I said, "I knew you couldn't arrest me for yelling in my own car. You haven't heard the last of this." The officer replied, "I didn't arrest you for shouting in your car. I was directly behind you at the light. I saw you screaming and beating your steering wheel, and I said to myself, "what a jerk, "but there was nothing I could do for throwing a fit in your own car. Then I saw the CROSS hanging from your rear view mirror, the bright yellow "CHOOSE LIFE" license tag and the "JESUS IS COMING SOON" bumper sticker, and **I thought you must have stolen the car."**

POINT MADE?

Chapter Four Introduction

◇<

I really had a hard time with the working of my faith until I realized through the Holy Spirit that it is not faith in me or my abilities, but in God, His abilities and willingness to heal. So, I took my eyes off me and put them on God where they belong.

Forsaking All, I trust Him

Faith

FAITH COMES BY.........

1. Hearing,
2. Looking,
3.Receiving
4. Believing

Smith Wigglesworth was famous for saying, "Only Believe"

Our actions are a statement of our faith

Actions and reactions are grounded on and released through our faith

The Ant and the contact lens
A true story by Josh and Karen Zarandona

GOD IS NOT LIMITED BY OUR THINKING OR OUR ABILITIES

Chapter Four

Faith is in God, not your ability faith through choice and through doing

◇◁

Forsaking All, I trust Him
Faith

A belief in and a confident attitude toward Him and His goodness. Including a commitment to His will for your life. In Heb 11, Abel, Enoch, Noah, Abraham, Sarah, Isaac, Jacob, Joseph and Moses are described as living by faith and the prophet Habakuk taught that "the just shall live by faith." (Hab 2:4)

An intellectual agreement with the "Word of God " is not enough but it is the beginning. meaning you read the scripture then you think it out, place yourself in agreement by speaking it out then your mind sets itself up against anything that does not agree.

If I need a healing in my body I look for a scripture that most closely fits the answer to my need. I place myself in agreement by speaking it out then I take my stand in defense of the scripture. I am saying to myself and to God, I know my body has problems, but your "Word" says I have been healed by Jesus name and I claim the healing and choose to believe the truth of your "Word," no matter what my body or even the Doctors have to say about it.

You are free to treat the symptoms if you choose. Some do, some don't.

People go to hell and never know that Jesus prepaid their way to heaven. If you don't know what belongs to you, it won't do you any good. That's why God put teachers in the Church. That's why He gave us His "Word," to tell us what belongs to us. Take it to the Bank....Our Spiritual Bank. Faith is the conduit from God to us. It is the key that unlocks our blessings.

FAITH COMES BY.........

1. **Hearing,**
Rom 10:17 NKJV
17 So then faith comes by hearing, and hearing by the word of God.

Isa 55:3 NKJV
3 Incline your ear, and come to Me. Hear, and your soul shall live; And I will make an everlasting covenant with you — The sure mercies of David.

2. **Looking,**
Isa 45:22 NKJV
22 "Look to Me, and be saved, All you ends of the earth! For I am God, and there is no other.

3.**Receiving**
John 1:12 KJV
12 But as many as received him, to them gave He power to become the sons of God, even to them that believe on his name:

4. Believing NKJV
Matt 21:22
22 And whatever things you ask in prayer, believing, you will receive."

**Smith Wigglesworth was famous for saying,
"Only Believe"
Believe 247 times in the New Testament
Faith is found 244 times**

Forsaking All, I trust Him
Dr. R.A. Torrey, founder of the Montrose Bible Conference, in Montrose, Pa. gave this definition of faith.
Unhesitating Assurance, even though it is unsupported by any other evidence and even though everything seems against fulfillment. This faith is not blind faith. It rests upon a full knowledge of God as revealed through His word.

Matt 9:22 NKJV
22 But Jesus turned around, and when He saw her He said, "Be of good cheer, daughter; **your faith has made you well.**" And the woman was made well from that hour.

Matt 9:2 NKJV
2 Then behold, they brought to Him a paralytic lying on a bed. **When Jesus saw their faith**, He said to the paralytic, "Son, be of good cheer; your sins are forgiven you."

Matt 9:27-30 NKJV
27 Two Blind Men Healed
When Jesus departed from there, two blind men followed Him, crying out and saying, "Son of David, have mercy on us!" 28 And when He had come into the house, the blind men came to Him. And Jesus said to them, **"Do you believe**

that I am able to do this?" They said to Him, "Yes, Lord." 29 Then He touched their eyes, saying, "According to your faith let it be to you."

Heb 12:2 NKJV
2 looking unto **Jesus, the author and finisher of our faith**, who for the joy that was set before Him endured the cross, despising the shame, and has sat down at the right hand of the throne of God.

Acts 15:11 NKJV
11 But we believe that **through the grace of the Lord Jesus Christ we shall be saved** in the same manner as they."

Our actions are a statement of our faith

Num 13:1-3 NKJV
13:1 And the LORD spoke to Moses, saying, 2 "Send men to spy out the land of Canaan, **which I am giving to the children of Israel**; from each tribe of their fathers you shall send a man, everyone a leader among them." 3 So Moses sent them from the Wilderness of Paran according to the command of the LORD, all of them men who were heads of the children of Israel.

Num 13:17-33 NKJV
17 Then Moses sent them to spy out the land of Canaan, and said to them, "Go up this way into the South, and go up to the mountains, 18 and see what the land is like: whether the people who dwell in it are strong or weak, few or many; 19 whether the land they dwell in is good or bad; whether the cities they inhabit are like camps or strongholds; 20 whether the land is rich or poor; and whether there are forests there or not. Be of good courage. And bring some of the fruit of the land." Now the time was the season of the first

ripe grapes. 21 So they went up and spied out the land from the Wilderness of Zin as far as Rehob, near the entrance of Hamath. 22 And they went up through the South and came to Hebron; Ahiman, Sheshai, and Talmai, the descendants of Anak, were there. (Now Hebron was built seven years before Zoan in Egypt.) 23 Then they came to the Valley of Eshcol, and there cut down a branch with one cluster of grapes; they carried it between two of them on a pole. They also brought some of the pomegranates and figs. 24 The place was called the Valley of Eshcol, because of the cluster which the men of Israel cut down there. 25 And they returned from spying out the land after forty days. 26 Now they departed and came back to Moses and Aaron and all the congregation of the children of Israel in the Wilderness of Paran, at Kadesh; they brought back word to them and to all the congregation, and showed them the fruit of the land. 27 Then they told him, and said: "We went to the land where you sent us. It truly flows with milk and honey, and this is its fruit. 28 Nevertheless the people who dwell in the land are strong; the cities are fortified and very large; moreover we saw the descendants of Anak there. 29 The Amalekites dwell in the land of the South; the Hittites, the Jebusites, and the Amorites dwell in the mountains; and the Canaanites dwell by the sea and along the banks of the Jordan." 30 Then Caleb quieted the people before Moses, and said, "Let us go up at once and take possession, for we are well able to overcome it." 31 But the men who had gone up with him said, "We are not able to go up against the people, for they are stronger than we." 32 And they gave the children of Israel a bad report of the land which they had spied out, saying, "The land through which we have gone as spies is a land that devours its inhabitants, and all the people whom we saw in it are men of great stature. 33 There we saw the giants (the descendants of Anak came from the giants); and **we were like grasshoppers** in our own sight, and so we were in their sight."

Num 14:6-9 NKJV
6 But Joshua the son of Nun and Caleb the son of Jephunneh, who were among those who had spied out the land, tore their clothes; 7 and they spoke to all the congregation of the children of Israel, saying:"The land we passed through to spy out is an exceedingly good land. 8 If the LORD delights in us, then He will bring us into this land and give it to us, 'a land which flows with milk and honey.' 9 Only do not rebel against the LORD, nor fear the people of the land, for they are our bread; their protection has departed from them, and **the LORD is with us**. Do not fear them."

Actions and reactions are grounded on and
released through our faith
Either you believe God or you don't
Choosing to believe Him is your first step

The Ant and the contact lens
A true story by Josh and Karen Zarandona

Brenda was a young woman invited to go rock climbing. Although she was very scared, she went with her group to a tremendous granite cliff. In spite of her fear, she put on her gear, took a hold on the rope and started up the face of the rock. well, she got to a ledge where she could take a breather. As she was hanging on there, the safety rope snapped against Brenda's eye and knocked out her contact lens.

Well, here she is, on a rock ledge, with hundreds of feet below her and hundreds of feet above her. Of course, she looked and looked and looked, hoping it had landed on the ledge, but it just wasn't there. Here she was, far from home, her sight now blurry. She was desperate and began to get upset, so she prayed to the Lord to help her find it. When she got to the top a friend helped her examine her eye and her clothing for the lens, but there was no contact lens to be found. She sat down, despondent, with the rest of the party, waiting for the rest of them to make it up the face of the cliff. She looked out at range after range of mountains thinking of that Bible verse that says, "The eyes of the Lord run to and fro throughout the whole earth." She thought, "Lord, you see all these mountains. You know every stone and leaf and you know exactly where my contact lens is. Please help me."

Finally, they walked down the trail to the bottom. At the bottom there was a new party of climbers just starting up the face of the cliff. One of them shouted out, "Hey you guys! Anybody lose a contact lens?" Well, that would be startling enough, but do you know why the climber saw it? An Ant was moving slowly across the face of the rock, carrying it on his back. Brenda told me that her father is a cartoonist, when she told him the incredible story of the Ant, The prayer, and the contact lens, he drew a picture of an Ant lugging that contact lens with the words, "Lord I don't know why you want me to carry this thing, I can't eat it and it is awfully heavy. But **if this is what you want me to do, I'll carry it for you.**"

GOD IS NOT LIMITED BY OUR THINKING OR OUR ABILITIES

Chapter Five introduction

◇<

Responsibility
Satan's games to keep you from praying
Use scripture to empower your prayers

Chapter Five

Responsibility

◇<

The new Christian has a lot of insecurities about praying for others. It is alright if done in private because if you make an error it is between you and the Father. This is a trick of Satan to keep you from stepping out in the things of God. God judges the heart and He already knows your heart is right. Tell the person you are about to pray with that you are new at praying with others. They will understand.

Before I became a Christian I had a man and wife team of doctors. Between the two of them I almost died. I was so sick I went to the Hospital Emergency Room and refused to leave. They finally admitted me and found out through a mandatory chest x-ray that I had bilateral pneumonia with a collapsed lung and also I had coughed so hard I had thrown a disc out of my back.

After I became a Christian I asked God, "Please remove them before they kill someone!"

After a couple months I heard that one of them had died, then a very short time later I heard the other one had died. Well, Satan had a hay day with me over that. He had me believing that it was my prayer that had done it. Right away I was afraid to pray any more.

God led me into an intercessory prayer group that were seasoned Christians. I watched and they encouraged me, also teaching me warfare. I learned to pray effectively. They operated from a knowing of who they were in Christ. I learned to be comfortable praying for others and I learned to incorporate scripture into my prayers. I also bought a book that helped me tremendously. Prayers that availeth much.

At another intercessory prayer group I was walking around praying in the Spirit when across the room I saw Angels sitting around waiting for me to pray so they could go out and get the answers. I prayed and said, "Lord, I need help with my finances." slowly the Angels got up, void of any energy or enthusiasm and went out to get the answer. I heard, "BORING." Then I said, "Father, I need help with my finances. Your word says,....when I tithe and give gifts, you will bring it back to me, pressed down, shaken together and pour out to me blessings I can't contain. Thank you Father for my blessings." With that those Angels lifted up, filled with power and supernatural energy and shot out like a bullet to retrieve the finances I had asked for.

The Holy Spirit spoke to me and said, "Now, which way do you want your prayers answered?" DUH!

I read..............................Jesus said,...................

Mark 16:18 NKJV
18 they will take up serpents; and if they drink anything deadly, it will by no means hurt them; **they will lay hands on the sick, and they will recover.**"

Matt 10:1 NKJV
10:1 The Twelve Apostles
And when He had called His twelve disciples to Him, **He gave them power over unclean spirits, to cast them out, and to heal all kinds of sickness and all kinds of disease.**

Matt 10:7-9 NKJV
7 And as you go, preach, saying, 'The kingdom of heaven is at hand.' 8 **Heal the sick, cleanse the lepers, raise the dead, cast out demons.** Freely you have received, freely give.

Luke 4:18-19 NKJV
18 "The Spirit of the LORD is upon Me, Because He has anointed Me To preach the gospel to the poor; He has sent Me to heal the brokenhearted, To proclaim liberty to the captives And recovery of sight to the blind, To set at liberty those who are oppressed; 19 To proclaim the acceptable year of the LORD."

John 14:12-14 NKJV
12 "Most assuredly, I say to you, **he who believes in Me**, the works that I do he will do also; and greater works than these he will do, because I go to My Father. **13 And whatever you ask in My name, that I will do, that the Father may be glorified in the Son. 14 If you ask anything in My name, I will do it.**

Do and say what the Holy Spirit is directing. Don't copy other people and you will succeed.
According to these scriptures I concluded that it is my responsibility to GO and lay hands and it is God's responsibility to do the healing.

Chapter Six introduction

Authority

The general purpose of authority

The Holy Spirit thoroughly equips for every good work

Satan tricks us into defeating ourselves

Satan wants to steal your testimony, Kill your witness and destroy your faith

Spiritual warfare

Chapter Six

Authority

◇<

AUTHORITY. The power or right to perform certain acts without impediment. It is based on some form of law, whether divine, civil or moral. Supreme authority is God's alone (Rom 13:1), hence all human authority is derived.

The general purpose of authority

The general purpose of authority is to promote order in society. Christians are given the authority to become children of God (John 1:12) and have the right to pursue certain forms of behavior (1Cor 6:12) Ultimately all forms of authority will revert to God, who bestowed it (1 Cor 15:24-28)

Therefore GO

Matt 28:18 NKJV
18 And Jesus came and spoke to them, saying, "All authority has been given to Me in heaven and on earth.

Matt 28:19-20 NKJV
19 **Go therefore** and make disciples of all the nations, baptizing them in the name of the Father and of the Son and of

the Holy Spirit, 20 teaching them to observe all things that I have commanded you; and lo, I am with you always, even to the end of the age." Amen.

As the Father has sent me, I am sending you

John 20:21-22 NKJV
21 So Jesus said to them again, "Peace to you! As the Father has sent Me, I also send you." 22 And when He had said this, **He breathed on them,** and said to them, "**Receive the Holy Spirit.**

The Holy Spirit thoroughly equips for every good work
2 Tim 3:16-17 NKJV
16 All Scripture is given by inspiration of God, and is profitable for doctrine, for reproof, for correction, for instruction in righteousness, 17 that **the man of God may be complete, thoroughly equipped for every good work.**

Matt 10:1 NKJV
And when He had called His twelve disciples to Him, **He gave them power over unclean spirits, to cast them out, and to heal all kinds of sickness and all kinds of disease.**

He gave them authority over evil forces

Mark 6:7 NKJV
7 Sending Out the Twelve
And He called the twelve to Himself, and began to send them out two by two, and gave them **power** over unclean spirits.

Eph 6:11-12 NKJV
11 Put on the whole armor of God, that you may be able to stand against the wiles of the devil. 12 For we do not wrestle against flesh and blood, but against principalities, against

powers, against the rulers of the darkness of this age, against spiritual hosts of wickedness in the heavenly places.

God's authority is unconditional and absolute (Psa 29:12; Isa 40:1) Making Him supreme over nature and human history alike. From this intrinsic authority comes that of governments (Rom 13:1-7) employers (Eph 6:5-9) parents (Eph 6:1-4) Church Elders (Heb 13:7,17) and others in positions of power. Similarly The Angels function under divine authority (Luke 1:19-20) and evil spirits are also subject to God's power (Eph 6:11-12).

Jesus authority

John 17:1-3
17:1 Jesus Prays for Himself
Jesus spoke these words, lifted up His eyes to heaven, and said: "Father, the hour has come. Glorify Your Son, that Your Son also may glorify You, 2 as You have given Him **authority** over all flesh, that He should give eternal life to as many as You have given Him.

God gave this authority to wise and respected men
Because they had been with Jesus for three years, they knew what was expected of them. They had the right attitude and they knew what to do with the power that had been given to them.

Satan tricks us into defeating ourselves. God wants us to be wise to his cunning ways.

The thief does not come except to steal, and to kill, and to destroy

John 10:10 NKJV
10 The thief does not come except to steal, and to kill, and to destroy. **I have come that they may have life, and that they may have it more abundantly.**

**Satan wants to steal your testimony,
Kill your witness and destroy your faith**

The God of peace will crush Satan under your feet

The value of our authority rests on the power behind that authority! Jesus received that authority and passed it to us, (Matt 28:18) meaning that God Himself backs us. As a believer you now have a legal right to function as Jesus did while on this earth. He bought and paid for that right and He has given you the "power of attorney to function in His place of authority." Now go forth and face the enemy without fear.

What is authority?
When a policeman raises his hand to stop traffic, you stop. you don't question him, you just stop. Physically he is no different than any other person but that uniform say's authority. When you are Born Again you have a much more authoritative uniform on, but because you can't see it in the natural Satan has tricked you into believing he is the powerful one, but he is only the "Bully" on the block. He has no power over you unless you give it to him.

As a roaring Lion

1 Peter 5:8 NKJV
8 Be sober, be vigilant; because **your adversary the devil walks about like a roaring lion,** seeking whom he may devour.

James 4:7
7 Submit yourselves, then, to God. **Resist the devil**, and he will flee from you.

Eph 6:10-11 NKJV
10 The Whole Armor of God
Finally, my brethren, be strong in the Lord and in the power of His might. 11 Put on the whole armor of God, that you may be able to stand against the wiles of the devil.

Mark 1:27-28 NKJV
27 Then they were all amazed, so that they questioned among themselves, saying, "What is this? What new doctrine is this? For with authority He commands even the unclean spirits, and they obey Him." 28 And immediately His fame spread throughout all the region around Galilee.

Luke 9:1-2 NKJV
9:1 Sending Out the Twelve
Then He called His twelve disciples together and **gave them power and authority over all demons**, and to cure diseases. 2 He sent them to preach the kingdom of God and to heal the sick.

When Christ ascended He transferred His authority to the Church. He is the head of the Church and believers make up the body. Christ' authority has to be perpetuated=(performed) through His body which is on the earth. (In different letters of the Bible Paul uses the human body as an illustration of the body of Christ.)

Christ is seated at the right hand of the Father, the place of authority and we are seated with Him (Just as we are in Him, He is in us). From the Moment you become a "Born again" believer, you have been adopted into the family receiving all the legal rights as a family member.

At that very moment we inherit the name of Jesus Christ. **I believe Satan's greatest fear is when Born again believers come into the full knowledge of who they really are in Christ.**

Years ago I read about a man in a Kenneth Hagin book who was found dead in a small shabby room he rented for $3.00 a week. He had been a familiar sight on the streets of Chicago for about 20 years, always dressed in rags and eating out of garbage cans. When he wasn't seen for two or three days, concerned people went to look for him and found him dead in bed. An autopsy revealed that he had died of malnutrition, yet a money belt was found around his waist containing $23,000.

That man had lived in poverty, peddling newspapers for a living, yet he had money. He could have lived in the finest hotel room, ate the best food, instead of garbage. but he didn't use what belonged to him.

We need to know what belongs to us. (Hosea 4:6) God says, "My people are destroyed for lack of knowledge." God has made a way for us to have a good life, but it is our choice. Live in poverty or know what is yours and enjoy all the benefits.

There is power and authority in the scripture. Find it, speak it out and watch God bring it about.

**Spiritual warfare
Don't make the mistake of taking this
part of your training lightly**

These words of warfare are based on the sixed chapter of Ephesians and also Mat 6:19.

As the military has different ranks, so does the Satanic realm. We speak to the different ranks from the highest to the lowest. The following is the way I choose, but it can be done in other ways, as long as it is done according to scripture.

To me, Satanic interference is like Radio static, it is not to be feared but it needs to be removed so that you can receive a clear signal, In this case from God. I speak these words each morning and any other time I sense interference. Remember to do your warfare before going to do Ministry work.

Warfare

Satan, I bind you, your principalities, your powers, your rulers of darkness of this world, your spiritual wickedness in high places and all your demons. I command you to cease in your maneuvers against me. I break your chain of command over all the evil forces coming against me. I bind and cast all unclean spirits into the dry places and I bind you there. In the name of Jesus Christ of Nazareth Confusion to the enemy.

No soldier would go into battle unless he was fully armed and dressed for battle. The attitude of the soldier is equally important. He must walk in total confidence. The principles he is fighting for must be indelibly written in his mind and heart and he must know in whom he serves.

Dressed for Battle

I put on the whole armor of God. The breast plate of righteousness, the girdle of truth, the sandals of peace, the helmet of salvation, the shield of faith and the two edged sword of the Spirit which is the word of God in my heart.

Don't just say the words, think about what you're saying. You are covering yourself in the power and integrity of the word of God. "It is sharper than any two edged sword."

Matt 16:19 NKJV
19 And I will give you the keys of the kingdom of heaven, and whatever you bind on earth will be bound in heaven, and whatever you loose on earth will be loosed in heaven."

WE BIND GOD' HANDS BY NOT SPEAKING THE WORD.

James 4:7-8 NKJV
7 Submit yourselves, then, to God. Resist the devil, and he will flee from you. 8 Come near to God and he will come near to you.

Luke 11:24-25 NKJV
24 An Unclean Spirit Returns
"When an unclean spirit goes out of a man, he goes through dry places, seeking rest; and finding none, he says, 'I will return to my house from which I came.'

Satan will try to stop you. He will find any weakness you have and there will be times when you will say, "I wonder if it is worth it?" IT IS! you will begin to recognize his tricks. You will then be able to see them in other areas of your life. Your weaknesses will then become your strengths and pretty soon you will have Satan and his cohorts on the run. **Don't give up, get up and fight!**

Job 1:10 NKJV
10 Have You not made a hedge around him, around his household, and around all that he has on every side? You have blessed the work of his hands, and his possessions have increased in the land.

My original Spiritual Teacher
Curt Wise

My original Spiritual teacher, Curt Wise helped me to understand the Spiritual realm and how to recognize and protect myself from negative forces. I honor him as a brilliant teacher in the Holy Spirit. He taught me to put the Holy Spirit in His proper place in my Spiritual walk. He placed in me knowledge and practical information on how to use that knowledge in my everyday life.

While I was taking an offering at Church I experienced confusion. It was normal for the Holy Spirit to give me the words to speak, but this time I only received scripture. After the service Curt came up and asked, "Did you have a rough time with the offering?" and I asked, "Was it that obvious?" He replied, "not to most. Did you notice the young man sitting in the front row with the preachers daughter? He used to take the offering here and he was having a problem with jealousy." (jealousy is a negative force.)

He made me aware of how these negative forces effect us. He said, "when you are in a room full of people and someone yells **FIRE!** Fear hits everyone and they all run toward the doors. It is the same with all negative emotions like fear, hate, anger and jealousy."

When these emotions are active they wash over on you. If someone enters the room you're in and they are angry, you actually feel it. I have experienced confusion from it so now I put up a hedge of protection around me every day.

I put up a hedge of protection around me, between me and all negative forces coming from anywhere. (Job 1:10) In Jesus name.

I also do this when I go into Hospitals, Jails, Churches, Other people's homes or businesses I also say, "I bind all transfer of spirits." When I go to pray for others.

Chapter Seven Introduction

✧

The Holy Spirit
The Answer Man

Walk and live in the Holy Spirit

Holy Spirit
(God's Power in Action)

The Spirit of Truth

Chapter Seven

The Answer Man

Ask direct questions / Don't just pray

❤

The Holy Spirit

1 Cor 2:1-16 NKJV

2:1 And I, brethren, when I came to you, did not come with excellence of speech or of wisdom declaring to you the testimony of God. 2 For I determined not to know anything among you except Jesus Christ and Him crucified. 3 I was with you in weakness, in fear, and in much trembling. 4 And my speech and my preaching were not with persuasive words of human wisdom, but **in demonstration of the Spirit and of power**, 5 that your faith should not be in the wisdom of men but in the power of God.

6 However, we speak wisdom among those who are mature, yet not the wisdom of this age, nor of the rulers of this age, who are coming to nothing. 7 But **we speak the wisdom of God** in a mystery, the hidden wisdom which God ordained before the ages for our glory, 8 which none of the rulers of this age knew; for had they known, they would not have crucified the Lord of glory.

9 But as it is written: "Eye has not seen, nor ear heard, nor have entered into the heart of man the things which God has prepared for those who love Him." 10 But God has revealed them to us through His Spirit. For the Spirit searches all things, yes, the deep things of God. 11 For what man knows the things of a man except the spirit of the man which is in him? Even so no one knows the things of God except the Spirit of God. 12 Now we have received, not the spirit of the world, **but the Spirit who is from God, that we might know the things that have been freely given to us by God.**

The truths of God that the Holy Spirit reveals are freely given, but you must spend time with Him to receive them. The time you spend now will forever pay dividends. The goal of the time spent with Him is to draw closer to Him and to learn to recognize His voice.

1 Cor 2:13 NKJV
13 These things we also speak, not in words which man's wisdom teaches but which the Holy Spirit teaches, comparing spiritual things with spiritual.

The Holy Spirit does not dictate to us the way Satan does, He teaches us.

14 But the natural man does not receive the things of the Spirit of God, for they are foolishness to him; nor can he know them, because they are spiritually discerned.
We can't expect unsaved people to understand the things of God because they don't have the Spirit of God to teach them. Spiritual things are Spiritually discerned.

15 But he who is spiritual judges all things, yet he himself is rightly judged by no one.

16 For "who has known the mind of the LORD that he may instruct Him?" **But we have the mind of Christ.**

Every Born Again Spirit filled believer has within them all the power they will ever need to get them through whatever circumstances or situations they will ever encounter.

Holy Spirit
(God's Power in Action)

Omnipotent Luke 1:35	**All Powerful**	
Omniscient	1 Cor 2:10,11	**All Knowing**
Omnipresent	Psa 139:13-17	**Present Everywhere**
Creator	Gen 1:2	
Sovereign	1 Cor 2:6,11	
Indwells	Rom 8:11	
Anoints	1 John 2:20	
Baptizes	Acts 2:17-41	
Guides	John 16:13	
Empowers	Mic 3:8	
Sanctifies	Rom 15:16	**Set Apart**
Bare' witness	Rom 8:16	
Helps	John 14:16-26	
Gives Joy	Rom 14:17	
Gives Discernment	1 Cor 2:10-16	
Bears fruit	Gal 5:22	**Are Holy Spirit Taught**
Gives Gifts	1 Cor 12:3-11	
Comforts	Acts 9:31	
Illuminates the mind	1 Cor 2:12-13	
Reveals thing of God	Isa 40:13,14	

The Holy Spirit will empower you for whatever you need as long as it is NOT against scripture.

The Spirit of Truth

John 16:13-15 AMP
13 But when He, the Spirit of Truth (the Truth-giving Spirit) comes, He will guide you into all the Truth (the whole, full Truth). For He will not speak His own message [on His own authority]; but He will tell whatever He hears [from the Father; He will give the message that has been given to Him], and He will announce and declare to you the things that are to come [that will happen in the future]. 14 He will honor and glorify Me, because He will take of (receive, draw upon) what is Mine and will reveal (declare, disclose, transmit) it to you. **15 Everything that the Father has is Mine. That is what I meant when I said that He [the Spirit] will take the things that are Mine and will reveal (declare, disclose, transmit) it to you.**

Walk and live in the Holy Spirit

Gal 5:16-25 AMP
16 But I say, **walk and live [habitually] in the [Holy] Spirit [responsive to and controlled and guided by the Spirit]**; then you will certainly not gratify the cravings and desires of the flesh (of human nature without God). 17 For the desires of the flesh are opposed to the [Holy] Spirit, and the [desires of the] Spirit are opposed to the flesh (godless human nature); for these are antagonistic to each other [continually withstanding and in conflict with each other], so that you are not free but are prevented from doing what you desire to do. 18 But if you are guided (led) by the [Holy] Spirit, you are not subject to the Law. 19 Now the doings (practices) of the flesh are clear (obvious): they are immorality, impurity, indecency, 20 Idolatry, sorcery, enmity, strife, jealousy, anger (ill temper), selfishness, divisions (dissensions), party spirit (factions, sects with peculiar opinions, heresies),

21 Envy, drunkenness, carousing, and the like. I warn you beforehand, just as I did previously, that those who do such things shall not inherit the kingdom of God. 22 But the fruit of the [Holy] Spirit [the work which His presence within accomplishes] is love, joy (gladness), peace, patience (an even temper, forbearance), kindness, goodness (benevolence), faithfulness, 23 Gentleness (meekness, humility), self-control (self-restraint, continence). Against such things there is no law [that can bring a charge]. 24 And those who belong to Christ Jesus (the Messiah) have crucified the flesh (the godless human nature) with its passions and appetites and desires. 25 If we live by the [Holy] Spirit, let us also walk by the Spirit. [If by the Holy Spirit we have our life in God, let us go forward walking in line, our conduct controlled by the Spirit.]

Make the path of the Spirit the place where you habitually live and walk. Become so comfortable walking in the Spirit you don't know where you leave off or where God begins.

It's time for us to take a giant step upward. Allowing our flesh to rule us is stupid on our part. We have the power of God at our disposal and all we have to do is connect. God is not going to do everything for us, we have to do our part. He says He will bless what we put our hand to.

Through the Holy Spirit

Through the Holy Spirit we can become the eyes, ears, hands and oracle for God. Don't think I am saying that you are a God. You are not, but you are the body walking around representing His love and will to heal them. The Holy Spirit is the key. Without His input you are ordinary. With Him and His leading you become supernatural. Which one do you want to be?

I will instruct you in how to access the mind of Christ in praying for others. At first it will be strange, even awkward to some but with practice and the proving you will be amazed at how your prayers take on the power that can only come from God. You will be so humbled by the result that you can't get puffed up.

This is not a game
Don't treat this as a game, It isn't. You are asking **Almighty God** to help you to help get people healed. You treat this with reverence in your heart. Knowing that God knows what is wrong with that person and how to heal them.

You begin by asking simple questions. I'm not a morning person so He started me with, "what should I wear today?" That was great because I was always content with what He told me and it was a safe question. Then it was "Holy Spirit what should I fix for supper?" What does this have to do with the healing Ministry? Everything. From there it was Holy Spirit how do I pray for this person? **Asking His opinion became a habit**.

Chapter Eight introduction

◇✕

Ministry etiquette

Types of healing

Laying on of Hands

Look to the Apostles and Prophets as your
example

The doctrine of laying on of hands

Set apart for service

Before praying for others, pray for yourself

Virtue (Power) flows one to another

Lay hands suddenly on no man

Anoint him with oil

The Art of Laying on of Hands

Gentleness

Ask the Holy Spirit

All The Fullness Of The Godhead

Getting personal

The Catcher

Chapter Eight

Do's and Don'ts in the Healing Room
or
Ministry etiquette

◇◁

It has been my good fortune to be associated with some professional performers and from listening to them I have gleaned from their experience (good and bad) certain Do's and Don'ts for those of us in the public eye. It is important for us to understand that we are very much in the public eye and though we are not paid performers, we are to behave professionally.

If you are an ambassador to the United Nations representing the United States you would act accordingly, and if the president got up to make a speech you certainly would not do anything disruptive or try to draw attention to yourself. **We represent Jesus the Christ, The anointed one and His anointing. The King of Kings. The name above all names, not just a president. He is our very foundation, our beginning and our end. Act accordingly.**

There will be only one person speaking at a time. The Holy Spirit is a gentleman and does not embarrass or interrupt the person speaking. When they are done you will have your time.

Make sure you are not talking to others in the Ministry team or doing anything to draw attention to yourself and away from the speaker. Remember that God is preparing their hearts and minds to receive from Him.

If you have any differences with anyone in the healing team it should be handled elsewhere, never to be brought out in the meeting. Your goal is to be the example to follow, not the central figure of gossip because of unacceptable behavior at the expense of those who may be ready to accept the Lord Jesus as Savior.

Unity with each other and the Holy Spirit is essential, **not an option**. In order for the Holy Spirit to move freely we must be in unity. If we are not in unity it leaves an open door for Satanic interference, causing confusion and ultimately defeating the purpose for our being there. Our behavior may make the difference between someone receiving their healing or Jesus as their Savior. Personally I don't want to be held accountable for someone going to hell or living in pain for the rest of their lives.

Remember, when you walk into that meeting, you are a Minister of God, act like it. We have an opportunity to make a real difference in the lives of those who come to us so use that time wisely. Don't leave room for the flesh. **Don't let Satan use you to rob those in need and don't quench the Holy Spirit.**

Types of Healing

Before you begin Ministering you should know that there are two types of physical healing. There is healing that is gradual and there are miracle healings that are instant. There is also spiritual, emotional and mental healings. I would love to have every person healed instantly but it is not up to me, it is God's call. That's what makes Him God. Whether we see it or not they receive every time we lay hands on them.

Laying on of hands
(your hands-His hands)

HANDS, LAYING ON OF

The placing of hands upon a person by a body of believers in ceremonial fashion to symbolize that person's authority or his appointment to a special task.

The practice of laying hands on someone or something occurs frequently in the Old Testament-particularly the laying of hands on the head of an animal intended for sacrifice. In the account of the ritual of the Day Of Atonement, the priest laid his hands on the Scapegoat (Lev 16:12). This probably symbolized the transferral of the sins and guilt of the people to the goat, which was taken away into the wilderness.

In the New Testament Jesus laid his hands on children (Matt 19:13,15) and on the sick when he healed them (Matt 9:18). In the early church the laying on of hands was also associated with healing, the reception of the Holy Spirit (Acts 9:17), the setting apart of persons to particular offices and work in the church (Acts 6:6), the commissioning of Barnabas and Paul as missionaries (Acts 13:3), and the setting apart of Timothy (1 Tim 4:14; 2 Tim 1:6). The ritual was accompanied by prayer (Acts 6:6).

The laying on of hands was not a magical or superstitious rite that gave a person special power. It expressed the idea of being set apart by the entire church for a special task.

Hands

In consecration   In prayer   In healing   In blessing children

Lifted up in benediction   In ordaining the Levites
In solemnizing testimony

(from Nelson's Illustrated Bible Dictionary, Copyright ©
1986, Thomas Nelson Publishers)

Look to the Apostles and Prophets as your example

Eph 2:19-22 NKJV
19 Now, therefore, you are no longer strangers and foreigners,
but fellow citizens with the saints and members of the household of God, 20 **having been built on the foundation of
the apostles and prophets, Jesus Christ Himself being the
chief cornerstone,** 21 in whom the whole building, **being
fitted together, grows into a holy temple in the Lord,** 22 in
whom you also are being built together for a dwelling place
of God in the Spirit.

The doctrine of laying on of hands

Heb 6:1-3 NKJV
6:1 Therefore, leaving the discussion of the elementary principles of Christ, let us go on to perfection, not laying again
the foundation of repentance from dead works and of faith
toward God, 2 of **the doctrine** of baptisms, **of laying on of
hands,** of resurrection of the dead, and of eternal judgment.

These are all foundation beliefs.

Set apart for service
Acts 13:1-3 KJV3:1 Now there were in the church that was
at Antioch certain prophets and teachers; as Barnabas, and

Simeon that was called Niger, and Lucius of Cyrene, and Manaen, which had been brought up with Herod the tetrarch, and Saul. 2 As **they ministered to the Lord,** and fasted, the Holy Ghost said, **Separate me Barnabas and Saul for the work whereunto I have called them.** 3 And when they had fasted and prayed, **and laid their hands on them,** they sent them away.

All Christians are called to pray and lay hands on the sick, but not all are called to the healing Ministry. If you are, God will witness it to you. You can still be a part of the healing team because everyone should learn to pray and lay hands on the sick. I know Ministers who need to learn.

Before praying for others, pray for yourself

Father,

Please forgive me for all sins, known and unknown, I forgive everyone who has trespassed against me. If there is anything in me that is offensive to you please cause me to change it. I submit to you all that I am and all that I will be. In Jesus Name

Holy Spirit please give me the words to speak. You words not mine and prepare his/her heart to receive his/her healing. I will give you all the glory. In Jesus Name

Virtue (Power) flows one to another

Mark 5:29-30 NKJV

29 Immediately the fountain of her blood was dried up, and she felt in her body that she was healed of the affliction. 30 And Jesus, immediately knowing in Himself that **power had gone out of Him,** turned around in the crowd and said, "Who touched My clothes?"

It is believed that the Hem of His garment was referring to His Prayer Shawl.

Lay hands suddenly on no man

1 Tim 5:22 KJV
22 Lay hands suddenly on no man, neither be partaker of other men's sins: keep thyself pure.

Some people get hostile if you touch them. You don't want to find out the hard way. Others are very protective and don't like certain areas touched. Some have pain in their bodies and it hurts. Some have unclean spirits that you don't want any part of. Simply ask God if or where to touch that person. It's an easy way to stay out of trouble.

Anoint him with oil

James 5:14-16 NKJV
14 Is anyone among you sick? Let him **call for the elders of the church, and let them pray over him, anointing him with oil in the name of the Lord.** 15 And the prayer of faith will save the sick, and the Lord will raise him up. And if he has committed sins, he will be forgiven. 16 Confess your trespasses to one another, and pray for one another, that you may be healed. The effective, **fervent prayer of a righteous man avails much.**

How to Anoint him/her with oil
(The oil is a symbol the Holy Spirit' power)
First ask if you may anoint them, then put a small amount of oil on your finger, and touch their forehead. If you choose to, you can anoint their hands for the work of the Lord.
Say, "I anoint you for healing in the name of the Father, The Son and the Holy Spirit."

Be aware of what an honor it is to lay hands on God's chosen people. You are standing in proxy for Jesus. When you reach forth your hand to touch that child of God, you are the vessel chosen by God to be His hands. Do not take that lightly.

Common Sense
The Art of Laying on of Hands

0

Think of a three foot circle surrounding each person. It is his/her space. Respect it.

The touching of another person is very personal. Their body is **their** territory, so when they ask or agree to your touching it they trust you to do this with the greatest respect. They are actually opening themselves up to you and to the God you serve.

Gentleness
Be thoughtful and gentle. Be directed on where, when or if you should put your hands on them. He knows that person and how they will receive from Him. Always protect that person, they have entrusted themselves to you.

Don't mess up their hair.
Don't put them in a head lock.
Don't beat on their backs.
Don't shout in their ears.
Don't leave oil dripping all over them.

Ask the Holy Spirit

Ask the Holy Spirit for the words to speak over that person. I also ask for a discerning. He will show you problem areas and give you insight into the problems and also give you the healing words to speak. In the beginning it usually comes slow but after a time of using the gifts, you learn what to expect and it then becomes easier. Remember you are actively calling on the gifts of the Holy Spirit and also asking for God's input. :) **WOW!**....What a novel idea. :)

I speak these things.

John 8:28-29 NKJV
28 Then **Jesus said** to them, "When you lift up the Son of Man, then you will know that I am He, and that I do nothing of Myself; but as My Father taught Me, **I speak these things**.

Revealed to you, by my Father

Matt 16:17 NKJV
17 Jesus answered and said to him, "Blessed are you, Simon Bar-Jonah, for **flesh and blood has not revealed this to you**, but **My Father who is in heaven**.

The Spirit of the LORD who rested on Jesus, is now in you!

Isa 11:2-3 NKJV
2 The Spirit of the LORD shall rest upon Him, The Spirit of wisdom and understanding, The Spirit of counsel and might, The Spirit of knowledge and of the fear of the LORD. 3 His delight is in the fear of the LORD, And He shall not judge by the sight of His eyes, Nor decide by the hearing of His ears;

ALL THE FULNESS OF THE GODHEAD

Col 2:9 KJV
9 For in him dwelleth all the fullness of the Godhead **bodily.**

**Remember He is Omniscient, Omnipresent and Omnipotent,
and He lives in you!!!**

Getting personal
The Word say's... "they shall lay hands on the sick." You can simply touch on their arm if you are not sure or if their problem is in a personal area.

The Catcher
Protect, Protect, Protect

Train people to be catchers. Don't leave them helpless. I have seen people being prayed for who should have experienced the wonderful power of God flooding their bodies and taking them down in the Spirit but there was no one to catch them.

If you don't have a catcher you can stand them against a wall or in front of a chair or a pew. A person can be set on a chair or even set them on the floor and still go under the power of God. Use common sense.

Chapter Nine introduction

◇✕

Words

Do Not Gossip.

Attitude

Your Words Spoken in The Healing Room

Jesus is the Word

Chapter Nine

Words

◇◁

Most of our lives we speak words and never give it a second thought unless those words are spoken by someone else and they are hurtful, then we latch on to each one. Words have great power whether they are negative or positive. They can hurt, they can teach. They can lift up or tear down. They create good or they create evil. Whether you see it or not, they create pictures and tell stories about the speaker and about the receiver. The receiver of your negative words may forgive you but they know what came out of your mouth was in your heart.

Do Not Gossip.

THE BEST INTERPRETATION I KNOW
OF FOR GOSSIP IS.......

If the person you are talking to is not part of the problem or part of the solution, it is gossip.

Matt 12:36-37 NKJV
36 But I say to you that for every idle word men may speak, they will give account of it in the day of judgment. 37 **For by**

your words you will be justified, and by your words you will be condemned."

Phil 4:8-9 NKJV
8 Meditate on These Things
Finally, brethren, whatever things are true, whatever things are noble, whatever things are just, whatever things are pure, whatever things are lovely, whatever things are of good report, if there is any virtue and if there is anything praiseworthy — meditate on these things. 9 The things which you learned and received and heard and saw in me, these do, and the God of peace will be with you.

God has given a guide line in His Word to show us a new focus and to fill our hearts and minds with positive things. There was a song written years ago called, "Count your many blessings." When negative begins to overwhelm me, I try to do just that. By counting the good in my life I am refocusing my thinking. Then I begin thanking God for all the good He is accomplishing in me and in my life. Very shortly I begin to feel healing gratitude for all that's right in my world. **Satan lost again!!!! :)**

Attitude
You are ministering in the Name of Jesus. **Your hands are His hands.** You are operating in the **"Mind of Christ."** What that person says or does is confidential. You can share what the healing was but not their name or personal things unless you have permission to do so. Walk in integrity at all times. **Integrity is what you do when no one is watching**.

Your Words Spoken in The Healing Room
You are preparing that person mentally and Spiritually to receive their healing and teaching them not to lose it because of wrong thinking. You must never speak negative words

that remove faith. Words like, "If God heals you", There is NO" IF" it is "when God heals you."

Rom 10:9-10 NKJV
9 that if you **confess with your mouth the Lord Jesus** and **believe in your heart that God** has raised Him from the dead, you will be saved. 10 For with the heart one believes unto righteousness, and with the mouth confession is made unto salvation.

This set of Scriptures sets the pattern for your success, not just in the healing room but for your success or failure in your Christian walk.

Rom 10:9 that if **you confess with your mouth the Lord (Lord means Boss)**

Jesus is the Word

John 1:1-2 AMP
1:1 **IN THE beginning [before all time] was the Word (Christ)**, and the Word was with God, and the Word was God Himself. [Isa 9:6.] 2 He was present originally with God.

When you speak (confess) The Word, you are placing yourself in agreement with it and saying the Word is Boss. Even when your circumstances don't agree with it, "If the Word say's it, I say it."

Rom 10:10 For with the heart one believes unto righteousness, and with the mouth **confession is made unto salvation.**

Meaning, I will place myself in agreement with the Word of God and confess it until I actually see it.

Salvation...save
verb, meaning it is active, moving, full of power
1. **To rescue from harm, danger or loss. to set free from the consequences of sin; Redeem.**
2. **To keep in a safe condition; Safeguard.**
3. **To prevent the waste or loss of; conserve.**
4. **To set aside for future use; store.**
5. **to treat with care by avoiding fatigue, wear or damage.**

Gen 1:1-4 NKJV
1:1 **The History of Creation**
In the beginning God created the heavens and the earth. 2 The earth was without form, and void; and darkness was on the face of the deep. And the Spirit of God was hovering over the face of the waters. 3 Then **God said**, (confess)"Let there be light"; and there was light. 4 And God saw the light, that it was good; and God divided the light from the darkness.

The Spirit of God is hovering over you, waiting for you to speak the Word that creates. Before you speak, what is in your heart? If you already think you are poor, sickly and it will never be any different, it won't. Make a decision to change your thinking to line up with the Word of God. What do you have to lose except your illness. Even if you don't see it, refuse to think of yourself as sick, broke, helpless, etc.

Prov 15:1-2 NKJV
15:1 A Soft Answer Turns Away Wrath, But a harsh word stirs up anger. 2 The **tongue of the wise uses knowledge rightly**, But the mouth of fools pours forth foolishness.

Eph 4:29 NKJV
29 Let no corrupt word proceed out of your mouth, but what is good for necessary edification, that it may impart

grace to the hearers. 30 And **do not grieve the Holy Spirit of God**, by whom you were sealed for the day of redemption. 31 **Let all bitterness, wrath, anger, clamor, and evil speaking be put away from you, with all malice.**

Speak words that create an atmosphere of love, forgiveness and healing. Words like, Jesus, Love, faithfulness, Joy, peace, Gentleness, Patience, Holiness and trust.

Chapter Ten introduction

◇×

How successful are you planning to be?

What Does the word Compassion mean?

What does the word passion mean?

Your soul is your mind, your will and your emotions.

Prayer

Pray without ceasing

A successful prayer

Break down

Heart and Humility

Believe
Does not doubt in his heart

Chapter Ten

Prayer

◇<

How successful are you planning to be? The time you spend in prayer and in the Word of God will help to determine it.

What Does the word Compassion mean?

It is a deep awareness of suffering of another and the desire to relieve it.

What does the word passion mean?

It is a deep desire. Also an object of love.

When we have a passion for God then we will have compassion for His people. When we pray for others it must come from our hearts. Not just out of our mind and out of our mouth.

When I was a new Christian I would talk to God, telling Him everything. There were times that I would laugh out loud at how wonderful it is to be a Born again Christian. I felt so close to Him and so loved. I can remember saying to my Grandmother, "This joy of the Lord can wear you out."

Begin your day purposely focused on God. Remembering and speaking out your thanks for all the things He has done and will do for you. This is to remind you of all the times He has come through for you and your family, which increases your faith in His love, His abilities and willingness to be your Father provider and protector. As you begin this process it will cause true praise and thankfulness to pour forth from your heart.

Your soul is your mind, your will and your emotions.

Heb 4:12 NKJV For the word of God is living and powerful, and sharper than any two-edged sword, piercing even to the division of **soul and spirit, and of joints and marrow**, and is a discerner of the thoughts and intents of the heart.

Ps 25:1-2 NKJV To You, O LORD, I lift up my soul (mind, will and my emotions). 2 O my God, I trust in You;

Prayer
Prayer aligns us with God. We step out of our natural and into the Spiritual with Him. This is where we begin to know His presence and to grow in our love and our worship of Him.

This is a precious time of bonding, don't waste it in the negative. Focus on the positive and then all that negative that tries to overwhelm us every day won't be able to penetrate your armor of praise to the Father.

Ps 71:8 NKJV Let my mouth be filled with Your praise And with Your glory all the day.

Phil 4:4-8 NKJV 4 Rejoice in the Lord always. Again I will say, rejoice! 5 Let your gentleness be known to all men. The Lord is at hand. 6 Be anxious for nothing, but in everything by prayer and supplication, with thanksgiving, let your requests be made known to God; 7 and the peace of God, which surpasses all understanding, will guard your hearts and minds through Christ Jesus. 8 Meditate on These

Things Finally, brethren, whatever things are true, whatever things are noble, whatever things are just, whatever things are pure, whatever things are lovely, whatever things are of good report, if there is any virtue and if there is anything praiseworthy — meditate on these things.

A Conversation of the Heart

Prayer is a reverent petition to God. An act of communion with Him and Worship, devotion, confession, praise and thanksgiving. Most of all it is a conversation of the heart.

How we Pray for others

Rev. Bobbie Woods was once given a "Word of knowledge" from God saying, "Pray for that child as if he were your own, make it personal." Pray from your heart to begin with, then go beyond until it comes from the heart of God.

Pray without ceasing

1 Thess 5:17 NKJV says, " pray without ceasing. "

The closer we learn to walk with Jesus, the easier it becomes! When we fall in love, we can't wait to be with that person. That is how it is when we fall in love with Jesus. We want to talk or sing to Him going down the road. We include Him in everything we do. That is when we learn to be attentive to His voice. It is a natural progression of a real relationship with someone you love.

A successful prayer

Humble, Thankful Heart

1 Kings 3:6-15 NKJV
7 Now, **O LORD my God**, You have made Your servant king instead of my father David, **but I am a little child; I do not know how to go out or come in. 8 And Your servant**

is in the midst of Your people whom You have chosen, a great people, too numerous to be numbered or counted. 9 Therefore give to Your servant an understanding heart to judge Your people, that I may discern between good and evil. For who is able to judge this great people of Yours?" 10 The speech pleased the LORD, that Solomon had asked this thing. 11 Then God said to him: "Because you have asked this thing, and have not asked long life for yourself, nor have asked riches for yourself, nor have asked the life of your enemies, but have asked for yourself understanding to discern justice, 12 behold, I have done according to your words; see, I have given you a wise and understanding heart, so that there has not been anyone like you before you, nor shall any like you arise after you. 13 And I have also given you what you have not asked: both riches and honor, so that there shall not be anyone like you among the kings all your days. 14 So if you walk in My ways, to keep My statutes and My commandments, as your father David walked, then I will lengthen your days."

15 Then Solomon awoke; and indeed it had been a dream.

Break down

7 Now, O LORD my God

A. He knew who his God was. He was no stranger, He said, "My God." He owned that relationship. God was personal to him, and God recognized Solomon's heart and words because He knew that Solomon was His kid.

B. He then said, "but I am a little child; I do not know how to go out or come in." This shows he had a humble heart. He knew who had the power to accomplish the work, he also knew who possessed the wisdom and he recognized that this was God's people, not his own.

8 Your servant is in the midst of Your people whom You have chosen.

These were God's people, a great people. It was like Solomon reversed what most King's would say. They would say, "these are my people." Solomon knew he was the servant and the people were God's people and therefore a great people to be treated with respect.

9. give to Your servant an understanding heart to judge Your people.

Solomon was asking God to give him the tools for the job. He knew that without God he would fail.

When you are called to, or appointed to do a work by God, He wants you to ask Him for the tools to accomplish **His Ministry**. He designed the position and you are the servant chosen to do what He wants accomplished.

Heart and Humility

Heart... The inner self that thinks, feels and decides. In the Bible the word has a much broader meaning than it does in the modern mind. The heart is that which is central to man. The thinking process is carried out by the heart, it may think, understand, imagine, remember, be wise, and speak to itself. Decision making is also carried out by the heart. Purpose, intention and will are all activities of the heart. It is your true character or personality.

Humility...A freedom from arrogance that grows out of the recognition that all we have and are comes from God. Jesus is the supreme example of humility. He is completely adequate and of infinite dignity and worth. Biblical humility is not a belittling of oneself, but an exalting or praising of others, Especially God and Christ. A humble person therefore focuses more on God and others than on himself.

15. Then Solomon awoke; and indeed **it had been a dream**.
The beauty of this prayer is that it wasn't Solomon at all but God giving him the prayer to pray with the knowledge and focus of God's view on the subject. This is exactly what I want you to learn from the study.

If you ask, God will give you the knowledge, the tools and the questions to ask to accomplish the work **He is calling you to.**

Mark 11:22-25 NKJV **"Have faith in God**
22 So Jesus answered and said to them, **"Have faith in God.**
23 For assuredly, I say to you, whoever says to this mountain, 'Be removed and be cast into the sea,' and **does not doubt in his heart**, but believes that those things he says will be done, he will have whatever he says. 24 Therefore I say to you, whatever things you ask when you pray, believe that you receive them, and you will have them. 25 "And whenever you stand praying, **if you have anything against anyone, forgive him, that your Father in heaven may also forgive you your trespasses."** 26 But if you do not forgive, neither will your Father in heaven forgive your trespasses."

Does not doubt in his heart
Everyone has thoughts of doubt that run through their minds. Those thoughts don't cancel out your prayer. Just don't let those negative thoughts hang around long enough to get into your heart. Counteract the negative thought with the Word of God. Speak the "Word" then act like you have already received and begin to give God the Glory.

Chapter Eleven introduction

Prepare them to receive

Point of Contact

Healing Scripture

Rick Renner interprets healing from the Greek

Chapter Eleven

Prepare them to receive

Y ou must speak words of God's love in preparation for their healing. Speak the scripture that tells them they will receive their healing.

Example:
First, go up to them, meeting them with a smile and say, "Hi, my name is _____, Welcome to God's healing room."

Example Questions:
Do you know that God loves you?
Are you a "Born Again Christian?"
Have you ever received a healing before?
Do you have a favorite healing scripture?
What Church do you go to?
Have you been to our healing room before?
What is it that you want from God?

Explain your way of praying for their healing. I usually say, "I will ask God how to pray for you. I will only speak the words He gives to me. That could be two words or it could be many. I will ask you to say a simple prayer of forgiveness.

I do this with everyone because if you do not forgive, it puts a wall between you and God. The Word says you are healed and forgiven, but it also says if you do not forgive, He will not forgive you."

Point of Contact

Tell them that after you pray for them and say the words "In Jesus name" they are to consider that the point of contact. From that moment they must not allow any negative words about their healing to take root in their mind or heart.

The thoughts will come, but they must rebuke them by saying, "NO, I am healed by Jesus stripes."

Satan will come. He will try to steal their healing but if they say NO, and stomp their spiritual foot, and speak their chosen scripture he can't succeed. Then DON'T LET GO!

Some have said to me, "I feel like I'm lying when I say I'm healed." What I choose to say is, "My body may say, I'm sick, but I say I am healed by Jesus stripes, my body just doesn't know it yet."

Be friendly, but remember you are there for prayer. It's fine to talk longer if no one else is there waiting. If someone else is in the room praying, be considerate and leave the room if you want to talk longer.

Healing Scripture

This scripture was prayed by the Saints of old and they saw many miracles. That's good enough for me.

Luke 4:18-19 NKJV
18 "The Spirit of the LORD is upon Me, Because He has anointed Me To preach the gospel to the poor; **He has sent Me to heal the brokenhearted, To proclaim liberty to the captives And recovery of sight to the blind, To set at lib-**

erty those who are oppressed; 19 To proclaim the acceptable year of the LORD."

Matt 10:8-9 NKJV
8 Heal the sick, cleanse the lepers, raise the dead, cast out demons. Freely you have received, freely give.

Acts 4:29-30 NKJV
29 Now, Lord, look on their threats, and grant to Your servants that with all boldness they may speak Your word, 30 **by stretching out Your hand to heal, and that signs and wonders may be done through the name of Your holy Servant Jesus."**

Isa 53:4-6 NKJV
4 Surely **He has borne our griefs And carried our sorrows;** Yet we esteemed Him stricken, Smitten by God, and afflicted. 5 **But He was wounded for our transgressions, He was bruised for our iniquities;**
The chastisement for our peace was upon Him, And by His stripes we are healed. 6 All we like sheep have gone astray; We have turned, every one, to his own way; **And the LORD has laid on Him the iniquity of us all.**

Psalms 23:1-6 NKJV A Psalm of David.
The LORD is my shepherd; I shall not want. 2 He makes me to lie down in green pastures; He leads me beside the still waters. 3 He restores my soul; He leads me in the paths of righteousness For His name's sake. 4 Yea, though I walk through the valley of the shadow of death, I will fear no evil; For You are with me; Your rod and Your staff, they comfort me. 5 You prepare a table before me in the presence of my enemies; You anoint my head with oil; My cup runs over. 6 Surely goodness and mercy

shall follow me All the days of my life; And I will dwell in the house of the LORD forever

Rick Renner interprets healing from the Greek

Rom 8:26 KJV
26 Likewise the Spirit also helpeth our **infirmities:** for we know not what we should pray for as we ought: but the Spirit itself maketh intercession for us with groanings which cannot be uttered.

INFIRMITIES = ASTHENOS All diseases or sickness. All five categories are encompassed in this word. Including spiritual weakness.

1. NOSOS = All manner of disease that is a terminal condition with no known natural cure.
(Nosos is also the name of a demon god.)

2. MALAKIAN = Mark 4: Muscles, bones, nerves, crippling.

3. KAKOS = Vexed with demons. Mental illness.

4. MASTIGOS = Plague. Repeated torture. Issue of blood. Migraine, fungus, allergies. Like being whipped to the point of death, stop and when almost healed it takes place again.

5. ARROUSTOS = Mark 16:18 They are so physically ill they are comatose. They have no faith so Jesus has to use His.
I hope this excited you as much as it did me.

Chapter Twelve introduction

><

Agreement

Think about what you are allowing
yourself to become a part of

Agreement in prayer

Birds of a feather

Is sickness a punishment sent by God?

Diagnosis from a Doctor

Satan tricks us into defeating ourselves

Know what is yours and in whom you serve

Salvation

No Trespassing

Chapter Twelve

Agreement

Think about what you are allowing yourself to become a part of

Matt 18:18-20 NKJV
18 "Assuredly, I say to you, whatever you bind on earth will be bound in heaven, and whatever you loose on earth will be loosed in heaven. 19 **"Again I say to you that if two of you agree on earth concerning anything that they ask, it will be done for them by My Father in heaven. 20 For where two or three are gathered together in My name, I am there in the midst of them."**

Agreement in prayer

What are we agreeing to? Are you still hanging on that "Old Rugged Cross?" If you are, Jesus died for nothing. As for me, I was set free when He arose from the dead.

The Church you are attending

Are you in agreement with the Pastors way of teaching, thinking, treatment of the people?

Are they preaching from Grace or are they preaching guilt? We preach hard things but always teach ways to overcome. **Through God you can overcome anything in you that is not of Him.** When you go to Church do you feel like you have been beat up or do you feel empowered to face the world? Is your Pastor preparing you to "GO."

Are you associating with people who are putting your Pastor down or undermining their Ministry? **If you are BEWARE!!!!!**

Birds of a feather

Who are your friends? Would you want your child influenced by them? Are they Christians who are for real or in name only? Are they causing you to grow or are they causing you to fall away from the principles in the Word? **What is in the darkness will be brought to the light.** Don't do anything you will be ashamed of. As far as I am concerned you make Jesus a part of whatever you are a part of. Would He be in agreement with what you are subjecting Him to?

Is sickness a punishment sent by God?

The people of Old Testament times tended to think that sickness was a punishment for sin. This concept is explored fully in Job. Jesus was firmly convinced that His father's purpose for humankind was health, wholeness and salvation. Salvation provides for healing in every area of your life. Jesus did not teach that sickness was a punishment from God. Jesus was not only concerned for the physical healing, He also paid close attention to the mind and spirit of those who suffered.

Diagnosis from a Doctor

Do you automatically accept you are doomed or do you automatically **Think....**"nothing is impossible to my God.

I'm going to pass up this marvelous opportunity to accept defeat. I am blessed, I'm the BLOOD bought child of the LIVING GOD and my God always causes me to triumph. "

Do you hang on to comments that are said about you... She's pretty but she isn't too smart, or good looking, or spiritual. How about, you'll never learn, you're stupid, you're too old, too young, too fat, too skinny, you're not a good speaker, nobody likes you. Etc, etc, etc.

Comments that are made by you... he's a thorn in my side, he's a pain in my.........

He may become just that if you don't change your words.

Satan tricks us into defeating ourselves

If you don't know the "Word of God" or the way God does things you will fall for his tricks. God does not condemn, He corrects. **He is a good God.** He does not belittle or embarrass you. **He does not beat you up.** (Romans 8:1)

Words come at us all the time but we don't have to accept them. Words like,

Too young, too old, Ugly, poor, stupid, worthless, fat, shy, death, Dementia, Diabetes, Lung Cancer, Anemia, Leukemia, Lupus, Cancer, Heart Disease, Kidney Disease, Arthritis, etc.

I believe if I am in a group of people who have a negative personality and behavior, I should remove myself. That is not the behavior I want to operate in and if I stay around them long enough I will become a part of it.

I believe if I am in a Church that is controlling and does not treat the congregation with respect, I don't belong there.

If your favorite hangout is a place where they use the Lord's name in vain, you are placing yourself in agreement with what they are doing. No matter how many of my friends are there, It is not worth offending my Lord.

Where you choose to fellowship, right or wrong you are placing yourself in agreement with what they are doing and as such you are answerable to God.

There are times that negative things do happen, when you have no power over the situation. When that happens speak to God quietly saying, "I take myself out of agreement with that. In Jesus Name."

Know what is yours and in whom you serve

**Salvation...save Verb... An action word. It never stands still, it's on the move, it's energized,
full of power leading you toward becoming everything you can become through Jesus Christ, our Savior.**

1. **To rescue us from harm, danger or loss.
to set us free from the consequences of sin; to Redeem us.**
2. **To keep us in a safe condition; Safeguard.**
3. **To prevent the waste or loss of; to conserve us.**
4. **To set aside for future use; store.**
5. **to treat us with care by avoiding fatigue, wear or damage.**

**No Trespassing
Because it is written and I believe!**

Matt 16:23 NIV
23 Jesus turned and said to Peter, "**Get behind me, Satan!** You are a stumbling block to me; you do not have in mind the things of God, but the things of men."

James 5:14-16 NIV
14 Is any one of you sick? He should call the elders of the church to pray over him and anoint him with oil in the name of the Lord. 15 And the prayer offered **in faith** will make the **sick person well; the Lord will raise him up.** If he has sinned, he will be forgiven.

Ps 107:20 NKJV
20 **He sent His word and healed them, And delivered them from their destructions.**
Isa 53:4-5 NKJV
Surely **He has borne our griefs** And **carried our sorrows**; Yet we esteemed Him stricken, Smitten by God, and afflicted. 5 But **He was wounded for our transgressions, He was bruised for our iniquities; The chastisement for our peace was upon Him, And by His stripes we are healed.**

Matt 8:16-17 NKJV
16 When evening had come, they brought to Him many who were demon-possessed. And He **cast out the spirits with a word,** and **healed all who were sick,** 17 that it might be fulfilled which was spoken by Isaiah the prophet, saying: "He Himself took our infirmities And bore our sicknesses."

Matt 12:15-16 NKJV
15 But when Jesus knew it, He withdrew from there. And great multitudes followed Him, and **He healed them all.**

Luke 4:40-41 NKJV
40 When the sun was setting, all those who had any that were sick with various diseases brought them to Him; **and He laid His hands on every one of them and healed them.** 41 And **demons also came out of many**, crying out and saying, "You are the Christ, the Son of God!" And He,

rebuking them, did not allow them to speak, for they knew that He was the Christ.

Ps 23:1 NKJV
The LORD is my shepherd; I shall not want. 2 He makes me **to lie down in green pastures; He leads me beside the still waters.** **3 He restores my soul; He leads me in the paths of righteousness** For His name's sake. 4 Yea, though I walk through the valley of the shadow of death, **I will fear no evil; For You are with me;** Your rod and Your staff, they **comfort me.** 5 You prepare a table before me in the presence of my enemies; You **anoint my head with oil;** My cup runs over. 6 Surely **goodness and mercy shall follow me All the days of my life; And I will dwell in the house of the LORD Forever.**

Chapter Thirteen introduction

❖

You are Priceless

A reality check

The measuring stick

Take this quiz

Chapter Thirteen

You are Priceless

⋈

I can't claim the next two stories, but they helped my thinking as a Christian. Satan would try to make me feel inferior. He would say things like, "Who do you think you are, God is not going to work through you. You are a nobody and we know what your background is."

I don't know who the authors are but I sure appreciate their encouraging words.

Priceless

A well known speaker started off his seminar by holding up a $20.00 bill, In the room of 200, he asked, "Who would like this $20 bill? Hands started going up. He said, I am going to give this $20 bill to one of you, but first, let me do this." He proceeded to crumple the bill up, He then asked, " Who still wants it?" Still the hands were up in the air. Well he replied, "What if I do this? " He dropped it on the floor and started to grind it into the floor with his shoe. He picked it up, now crumpled and dirty. Now, "Who still wants it?" Still the hands went up in the air. "My friends, we have all learned a very valuable lesson. No matter what I did to the money, you still wanted it because it did not decrease in value. It was still worth $20." Many times in our lives we are dropped, crumpled and ground into the dirt by the decisions we make and the circumstances that come our way. We feel as though we are worthless, but no matter what has happened or what will happen, you will never lose your value: Dirty or clean, crumpled or finely creased, you are still priceless to those who love you. The worth of our lives comes not in what we do or who we know, but in WHO WE ARE.

A reality check

If someone were hired to write the story of your life, what would they have to say about you? If they interviewed your family, friends, co-workers, neighbors and those you have Ministered to, What story would they tell about you? How would your children rate you as a parent? Will your motives for serving God pass the test when you stand before Him? Do you judge others with the same measuring stick you use to judge yourself? Are you moved with compassion when you see others in trouble? Have you made a real difference for the better in the life of someone else?

The measuring stick

1 Cor 13:4-8 NIV
4 Love is patient, love is kind. It does not envy, it does not boast, it is not proud. 5 It is not rude, it is not self-seeking, it is not easily angered, it keeps no record of wrongs. 6 Love does not delight in evil but rejoices with the truth. 7 It always protects, always trusts, always hopes, always perseveres. 8 Love never fails.

Do these words stir your inner most being when you read them? For me they are a reality check. I would love to say I live up to these words of God, but I don't. I know I'm not doing everything I should, but I am trying. God forgives us for our shortcomings, but keep in mind that He said, we are to be hot and not cold. We may not be able to do everything but we can do some things. We can make a difference in the lives of others. Through Jesus Christ we can help others not because you have to, but as a natural progression of loving Jesus and wanting others to experience that same love.

Take this quiz

I got this quiz off the internet.
1. Name the five wealthiest people in the world.
2. Name the last five Heisman trophy winners.
3. Name the last five winners of the Miss America contest
4. Name the ten people who won the Nobel or Pulitzer prize.

How did you do?
The point is, none of us remember the head liners of yesterday. These are no second rate achievers. They are the best in their fields, but the applause dies. Awards tarnish. Achievements are forgotten.

1. List a few teachers who aided your journey through school.
2. Name three friends that have helped you through a difficult time.
3. Name five people who have taught you something worthwhile.
4. Name five people you enjoy spending time with.
Easier?

The lesson?
The people who make a difference in your life are not the ones with the most credentials, the most money, or the most awards. They are the ones who care. **Like you.**

Chapter Fourteen Introduction

◇×

Cheat Sheet

Before praying for others

Warfare

Chapter Fourteen

Cheat Sheet

◇<

Before praying for others

Father,

Please forgive me for all sins, known and unknown. I forgive all those who have trespassed against me. If there is anything in me that is offensive to you, please cause me to change it. I submit to you all that I am and all that I will be. In Jesus Name.

I put a hedge of protection around me. Between me and all negative forces coming from anywhere, and I bind all transfer of spirits.

Warfare

Satan, I bind you, your principalities, your powers, your rulers of darkness of this world, your spiritual wickedness in high places and all your demons. I command you to cease in your maneuvers against me. I break your chain of command over all the evil forces coming against me. I bind and cast all unclean spirits into the dry places and I bind you there.

In Jesus Name.   Confusion to the enemy.

Holy Spirit please give me the words to speak. Your words not mine and prepare his/her heart to receive his/her healing. I will give you all the glory. In Jesus Name.

Chapter Fifteen introduction

⬦✕

Cheat Sheet

The Salvation call

More Sample prayers

Chapter Fifteen

Cheat Sheet
The Salvation call

◇×

John 3:3&7 Say, **'You must be born again.'**

Firirst, **DON'T BEG!!!**
Your attitude must be positive. You are extending an invitation to join the most powerful, loving family available to mankind. When they accept that invitation show them your approval by welcoming them into the family.

Your scripture reference. John 3:3&7 Rom 10:9,10 Rev 3:20 II Cor 1:22

The following is a sample invitation to Salvation. It is only a guideline.

The Bible is a bi-lateral contract, meaning that each person making that contract is required to do something before it is binding.

John 3:3&7 Says, 'You must be born again.' and in

Rom 10:9,10
9 that if you confess with your mouth the Lord Jesus and believe in your heart that God has raised Him from the dead, you will be saved. 10 For with the heart one believes unto righteousness, and with the mouth confession is made unto salvation.

Which means that you believe that Jesus died and was resurrected from the dead for you.
Then in
II Cor 1:22 who (God) also has sealed us and given us the Spirit in our hearts as a guarantee.
and finally,
Rev 3:20-21
20 Behold, I stand at the door and knock. If anyone hears My voice and opens the door, I will come in to him and dine with him, and he with Me.

Now, I've said all this in order to help you understand that Jesus is here waiting for you to open the door of your heart to invite Him in. He wants you to make that contract so you can become one of His family members. If you choose to become His, you will then be asked to say a simple but life changing prayer asking Him to become your Lord. Lord means boss. If you have already spoken that prayer, it is not necessary to say it again, but if you haven't made that commitment we want you to have that opportunity now. If you have said that prayer before but you have fallen away from the Lord and you would like to pray a prayer of rededication, I would love to say that prayer with you. **Would you like to say that prayer?**

Heavenly Father, Thank you for the privilege of saying this prayer.

Ask,

Do you believe that Jesus came to earth, lived as a man and died on the cross for you?

Please repeat after me,

Father, please forgive me for all sins. I forgive all those who have trespassed against me.

Jesus, come into my heart and be the Lord of my life. Thank you Lord, I am a Born Again Christian.

Now, **Pray a prayer of blessing** over them, letting them know they are special in God's eyes.

Sit down and ask God to give you a prayer of Salvation, then study it and practice it until you are comfortable with it. Keep it with you to refresh your mind.

Chapter Sixteen introduction

❤

The ROOT, FRUIT and MOUNTAIN

Example prayer

Healing Scriptures

Chapter Sixteen

Healing Scriptures the ROOT, FRUIT and MOUNTAIN

◇<

R emember that you are being taught a process or formula for success in healing people God's way. You always ask the Holy Spirit to show you how to pray but what I am teaching you here is the way to speak to the problem after He has shown you what that problem is. The words "ROOT, FRUIT and MOUNTAIN is simply a word association to give you an easy way of remembering the formula.

ROOT means whatever the cause of the illness.
FRUIT means the results, symptoms or destruction caused by the illness in their body.
MOUNTAIN means anything that does not belong in your body to be removed.

SPEAK to the ROOT, the FRUIT
and to the MOUNTAIN
SPEAK..................

Prov 18:21 NKJV
21 **Death and life are in the power of the tongue,** And those who love it will eat its fruit.

Job 22:28 NKJV
28 You will also declare a thing, And it will be established for you; So light will shine on your ways.

Every prayer for healing must include a healing scripture. I usually begin with it, also every prayer for healing must conclude with, "In Jesus Name."
The Holy Spirit made me aware that whenever anything enters your body that is not of God, It causes confusion. That confusion is not of God.

SPEAK to the ROOT of the problem
When we pray, we can be told what the problem, prayer request is, and we can pray for it to be healed, but God has taught me to go beyond the obvious and speak directly to the root cause of the problem. We don't even have to know what the root is, we just speak to the root to be healed so it can't come back.

SPEAK to the FRUIT
Whatever disease that enters your body carries with it a fruit of its visit. We think of it as Symptoms or the destruction. Cancer, diabetes, lupus, etc. All carry a negative result of their presence.

SPEAK to the MOUNTAIN

Mark 11:23 NKJV
23 For assuredly, I say to you, **whoever says to this mountain, 'Be removed and be cast into the sea,'** and does not

doubt in his heart, but believes that those things he says will be done, he will have whatever he says.

We must speak to the problem to be removed. Don't pray for Jesus to remove it, you speak to it to be gone, In Jesus Name. You have the authority, Jesus gave it to you. **Now take it.**

The following are examples for you to get started. Don't get hung up in memorizing the words. learn the process and everything else will follow.

Example:
(opening)
Heavenly Father, You are the creator and the re-creator. There is nothing impossible to you. Thank you father that you always hear and answer our prayers. We come to you in the power and authority of the precious name of your Son, Jesus. Thank you for your word that heals.

(speak to the disease)
Cancer I command you to die by your very root. I speak to the confusion in this body to be removed. You have no hold on him/her and you are trespassing, be thou removed. I speak to the fruit of this invasion including the pain and all negative symptoms and I say you are replaced by the fruit of the Word of God. You are healed by Jesus stripes. Peace be still to this body and I bind all demonic interference. In Jesus Name I pray.

Diabetes I command you to die by your very root. I speak to the confusion and the root cause of this disease to be removed from this body. You have no hold on him/her and you are trespassing, be thou removed. I speak to the fruit of this destruction and I say Pancreas you are replaced by the fruit of the Word of God. You are healed by Jesus stripes. I bind all demonic interference. In Jesus Name I pray.

Heart Trouble Muscle, peace be still. All forms of obstructions be gone. I command you to pump perfectly for your body and to do the work that God created you to do. I speak life to you and I bind all forms of death from operating in you. Body receive your healing. You are healed by Jesus stripes. I bind all demonic interference. In Jesus Name I pray.

Blood Pressure II Tim 1:7 God has not given us a spirit of fear, but of power and of love and of a sound mind. All forms of stress, anxiety, worry, peace be still. I speak to all blood flow restrictions, you are removed safely from this body, healed and restored by Jesus stripes. I bind all demonic interference. In Jesus Name I pray.

Stroke I speak life to you and I bind all forms of death from operating in you. I speak to all blood flow restrictions, foreign matter, blood clots, you are removed safely from this body, healed and restored by Jesus stripes. I speak to the fruit of this destruction and to the root cause to be replaced by the fruit of the Word of God. Body receive your healing and be fully restored. I bind all demonic interference. In Jesus Name I pray.

Lupus I speak to the immune system and to all confusion and the root cause of this disease to be removed from this body, you are healed and restored. I command every organ in your body to receive your healing. I speak to the fruit of this destruction and I say all damage is replaced by the fruit of the Word of God. You are healed by Jesus stripes. I bind all demonic interference. In Jesus Name I pray.

Back Pain I command all Pain be gone. Whatever the root cause you are healed and restored. Vertebra's, disc, muscles, fluids, ligaments, bones and tendons, come into submission to God's Word and align yourself with this body. You are healed by Jesus stripes. I bind all demonic interference. In Jesus Name I pray.

Tooth Ache I command this Pain be gone. I speak to the root and nerves you are healed and restored. All swelling recede. Body come into submission to God's Word. You are healed by Jesus stripes. I bind all demonic interference. In Jesus Name I pray.

Head Ache I command this Pain be gone. Whatever the root cause you are healed and restored. Body come into submission to God's Word and align yourself with this body. You are healed by Jesus stripes. I bind all demonic interference. In Jesus Name I pray.

Broken Bone I command all Pain and residual weakness to be gone. I command the bones to align perfectly and to fuse and become even stronger than before. You are healed by Jesus stripes. I bind all demonic interference. In Jesus Name I pray.

Seizures Brain, come into unity and function perfectly. I command all confusion to be gone from you. Neurons, fire properly. I speak to the root cause of the Seizures, you are healed and restored. Body receive your healing. You are healed by Jesus stripes. I put up a hedge of protection between you and the negative pull of the moon and I bind all demonic interference. In Jesus Name I pray.

Bleeding I speak to this issue of Blood, cease in your maneuvers against him/her. I speak to the root cause of the bleeding you are healed and restored. Body receive your healing. You are healed by Jesus stripes. I bind all demonic interference. In Jesus Name I pray.

Paralyzed Death, you are released from your assignment against God's child. I speak to the block in the Motor control, be removed and function the way God created you ⁄ to function. I command the blood and feeling to flow properly and the muscles to be restored. You are healed by Jesus stripes, He took your infirmities and bare you sickness. I bind all demonic interference. Body receive your healing. Now walk. In Jesus Name.

Sinus I command this Pain be gone. I speak to the root cause of the problem to be healed. Swelling recede, air passages breath freely, mucus dry up. You are healed and restored. Body come into submission to God's Word. You are healed by Jesus stripes. I bind all demonic interference. In Jesus Name I pray.

Allergies I put up a hedge of protection between you and all negative forces that would hinder your body. I speak to the root cause of these allergies to be removed. I speak to the fruit of the allergic reaction to be replaced by the fruit of the Word of God. Healed by Jesus stripes. I bind all demonic interference. In Jesus Name I pray.

Cold /Virus I speak to the root cause of the problem to be healed. Swelling recede, air passages breath freely, mucus dry up. You are healed and restored. Body come into submission to God's Word. You are healed by Jesus stripes. I bind all demonic interference. In Jesus Name.

Blind, Deaf, Or Mute I speak to the root cause of this problem to be healed. Eyes, / ears, / mouth, be opened and function perfectly for your body. I speak creation and/or recreation where needed. You are healed by Jesus stripes He took your infirmities and bare you sickness. I bind all demonic interference. In Jesus Name.

Arthritis I command all Pain and residual weakness to be gone from this body. I speak to the root cause of the Arthritis to be healed. I speak to the destruction and the inflammation to be replaced by the fruit of the Word of God. You are healed by Jesus stripes. I bind all demonic interference. In Jesus Name I pray.

Fear II Tim 1:7 God has not given us a spirit of fear, but of power and of love and of a sound mind. All forms of stress, anxiety, worry, peace be still. I command all confusion to be gone from you. God is not the Author of confusion. I speak to the root cause of this fear to be healed and understanding to come. Mind come into submission to God's Word. You are healed by Jesus stripes. I bind all demonic interference from operating in you. In Jesus Name I pray.

Mental Illness II Tim 1:7 God has not given us a spirit of fear, **but of power and of love and of a sound mind.** All forms of stress, anxiety, worry, peace be still. I command all confusion to be gone from you. **God is not the Author of confusion.** Mind come into submission to God's Word. You are healed by Jesus stripes. I bind all demonic interference from operating in you. In Jesus Name I pray.

Bone / organ Transplant

I speak unity with the new organ / bone transplant in this body and I bind all forms of rejection. I bind all forms of death from operating in this body and I speak life to it. I bind all transfer of spirits from the donor. You are healed by Jesus stripes. I bind all demonic interference from operating in you.

Eye problems

I speak restoration to all parts and connecting tissue of this eye, including fluids, tissue and sight. You come into submission to the word of God, In Jesus Name I pray. You are healed by Jesus stripes. I bind all demonic interference from operating in you. In Jesus Name I pray.

Someone going to surgery I bind all spirits of death from operating in you. I speak life in you and health to you and your body and I bind all unclean spirits from operating in you.

Father, protect _____, surround him / her with your Holy Angels and cause every person that will touch him / her to have perfect hand, eye co-ordination and to see beyond their natural ability to see. You are healed by Jesus stripes.

DO NOT CAST SPIRITS OF ADDICTION OUT UNTIL THAT PERSON HAS GIVEN UP THE ADDICTION. When they come back saying they will never again partake, then cast the spirits out. In the interval **bind it from operating in that person.**

Drug / alcohol addiction I bind all unclean spirits from operating in you. In Jesus Name

Healing Scriptures

Isa 53:4-5 NKJV
4 Surely He has borne our **griefs And carried our sorrows; Yet we esteemed Him stricken, Smitten by God, and afflicted. 5 But He was wounded for our transgressions, He was bruised for our iniquities; The chastisement for our peace was upon Him, And by His stripes we are healed.**

2 Tim 1:7 NKJV
7 **For God has not given us a spirit of fear, but of power and of love and of a sound mind.**

Matt 16:19 NKJV
19 And I will give you the keys of the kingdom of heaven, and **whatever you bind on earth will be bound in heaven, and whatever you loose on earth will be loosed in heaven."**

John 14:13 NKJV
13 And **I will do whatever you ask in my name, so that the Son may bring glory to the Father.**
Ps 107:20 NKJV
He sent His word and healed them, And delivered them from their destructions.

Matt 4:24 NIV
24 News about him spread all over Syria, **and people brought to him all who were ill with various diseases, those suffering severe pain, the demon-possessed, those having seizures, and the paralyzed, and he healed them.**

Matt 9:20-22 NIV
20 Just then a woman who had been **subject to bleeding for twelve years** came up behind him and touched the edge of his cloak. 21 She said to herself, "If I only touch his cloak, I will be healed." 22 Jesus turned and saw her. "Take heart, daughter," he said, "your faith has healed you." And the woman was healed from that moment.

Matt 12:22 NIV
22 Then they brought him a **demon-possessed** man who was **blind and mute**, and Jesus healed him, so that he could both talk and see.

Mark 1:34 NIV
34 and **Jesus healed many who had various diseases.**

Mark 6:13 NIV
13 They drove out many demons and **anointed many sick people with oil and healed them.**

Acts 8:7 NIV
7 With shrieks, evil spirits came out of many, and **many paralytics and cripples were healed**

Prov 14:30 NKJV
30 A sound heart is life to the body, But envy is rottenness to the bones.

Isa 55:11 NKJV
So shall My word be that goes forth from My mouth; It shall not return to Me void, But it shall accomplish what I please, And it shall prosper in the thing for which I sent it.

Ex 23:25-26 NKJV
25 "So you shall serve the LORD your God, and He will bless your bread and your water. And **I will take sickness away from the midst of you. 26 No one shall suffer miscarriage or be barren in your land; I will fulfill the number of your days.**

References

Dr. R.A. Torrey, founder of the Montrose Bible Conference, in Montrose, Pa. Pg. 22

Trying to Do the Job Alone Author unknown
Received at Kenneth Hagins Ministers conference.

Man found dead. From a Kenneth Hagin book Pg. 30
Rick Renner interprets healing from the Greek Pg. 50 From his book, Sparkling Gems

Internet Stories
The Bumper Sticker Author unknown
The Ant and the contact lens A true story by Josh and Karen Zarandona
Take this quiz Author unknown

CPSIA information can be obtained at www.ICGtesting.com
Printed in the USA
LVOW080901201011

251254LV00002B/1/P